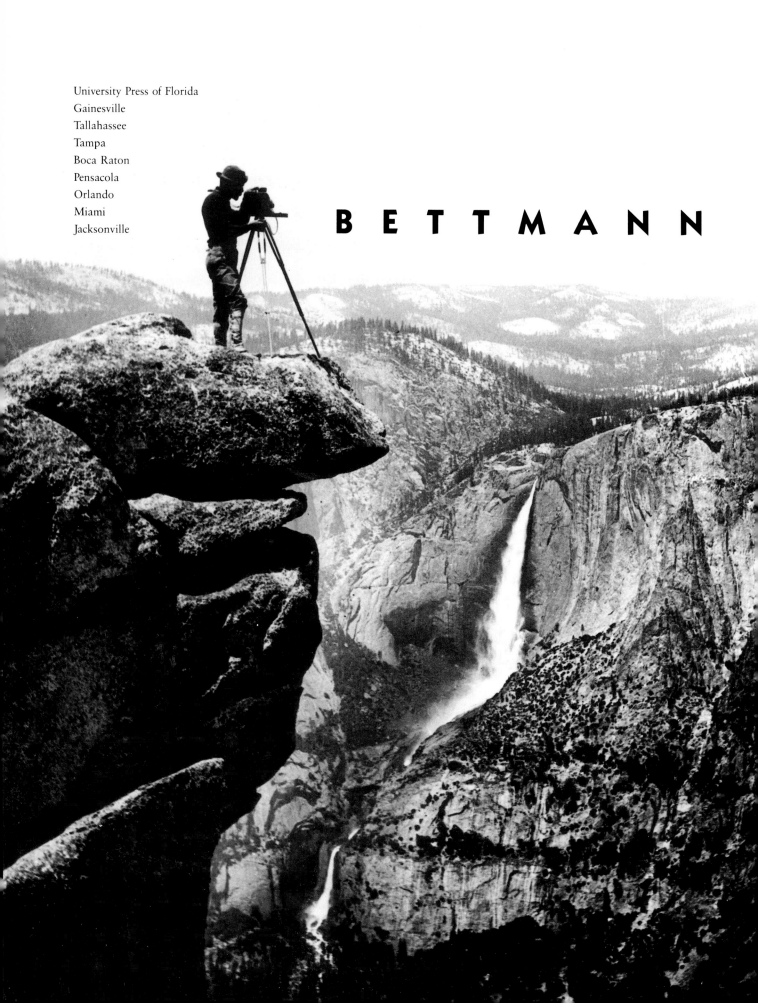

University Press of Florida
Gainesville
Tallahassee
Tampa
Boca Raton
Pensacola
Orlando
Miami
Jacksonville

BETTMANN

THE PICTURE MAN

Otto L. Bettmann

Skip Sheffield, Editorial Coordinator

Library of Congress Cataloging-in-
Publication Data

Bettmann, Otto.
Bettmann: the picture man / Otto L.
Bettmann ; Norman Sheffield, Jr.,
editorial coordinator.
p.   cm.
Includes index.
ISBN 0-8130-1153-1 (alk. paper)
1. Bettmann, Otto.   2. Photography
literature—Publishing—New York
(N.Y.)—History—20th century.
3. Photographs—Collectors and
collecting—New York (N.Y)—
History—20th century.
4. Photographs—Collectors and
collecting—United States—
Biography.   5. Publishers and
publishing—United States—
Biography.   I. Title.
Z473.B45   1992
381.45002′097471—dc20   92-10639

The University Press of Florida is the
scholarly publishing agency of the
State University System of Florida,
comprised of Florida A & M
University (Tallahassee), Florida
Atlantic University (Boca Raton),
Florida International University
(Miami), Florida State University
(Tallahassee), University of Central
Florida (Orlando), University of
Florida (Gainesville), University of
North Florida (Jacksonville), University
of South Florida (Tampa), and
University of West Florida (Pensacola).

University Press of Florida
15 Northwest 15th Street
Gainesville, FL 32611

CONTENTS

INTRODUCTION

Skip Sheffield

ONE DAY, THIRTY-FIVE YEARS into his career as founder and director of the Bettmann Archive, Otto Bettmann struck up a conversation with a fellow Westchester, New York, commuter. "Bettmann," the man muttered as they exchanged pleasantries. "Bettmann .... Are you somehow connected with the Bettmann Archive?"

"Connected?" Bettmann replied innocently. "I am absolutely *not* connected with the Bettmann Archive. I *am* the Bettmann Archive!"

While Dr. Bettmann had a perfect right to make his seemingly arrogant remark, rest assured he is no imperious King Louis XIV. More accurately, he is "immodestly modest"—a relentlessly hardworking scholar, author, and retired businessman who has had the good fortune to see a unique enterprise of his own invention grow and flourish into worldwide renown—all within the space of fifty years.

I can remember reading textbooks as a child and noticing the mysterious credit line "Bettmann Archive" beneath rare and evocative illustrations. What a wonderful and ancient place this Archive must be, I thought. In my childish fantasy I imagined a fortresslike edifice with towers, wrought iron gates, and perhaps even a moat protecting untold musty, priceless treasures. I assumed that Bettmann the founder had gone to his reward at the time of Queen Victoria's coronation, but I had no doubt his loyal descendants continued to work tirelessly, keeping the time-hallowed enterprise alive.

Imagine my surprise to discover as a journalist more than a quarter-century later that not only is Otto Bettmann alive and well and living in Boca Raton, but that the man himself laughs at the image of the Archive as an ancient, dusty place. "Years ago I remember a messenger asking, 'Is old Archie still around, and can I actually see him?'" he once told me with typical bemusement.

Yes, "old Archie" is still around, but his age has not brought complacency or reduced ambition. Indeed, Dr. Bettmann readily embraces the modern technology that has enabled the Bettmann Archive to flourish even after he relinquished the reins of it more than a decade ago. Furthermore, he spurns the past-worshipping cult of nostalgia that has been such a boon to his business.

There are few businesses in the United States so fully imprinted with the hand, mind, and spirit of a single man, a once-penniless, tenacious German immigrant, armed only with two trunks full of old pictures and an ambition to make it in America. The Bettmann Archive is now a division of a round-the-clock operation that, for a fee, dispenses pictures spanning from the dawn of time to the latest daily news photos from UPI and Reuters. The story of how Otto Bettmann "made it" is rich in drama and color. The more I learned about the man and his work, the more I became convinced that his story should be shared with others.

From the world of commerce, Dr. Bettmann has returned to his earlier love of books and scholarly research, serving as curator of special collections at Florida Atlantic University. As his story unfolds, three distinct elements begin to emerge. The first is the all-American tale of the poor but ambitious immigrant who, under extreme duress, abandoned his refined, cultured German home for an uncertain future in rough-and-tumble America. The story is underscored by the specter of pervasive anti-Semitism and growing Nazi oppression, yet uplifted by Bettmann's rapid assimilation into modern, progressive New York society.

The second part of the Bettmann saga falls into another typically American category: creating a new business and making a success of it. Though a scholar and historian first and foremost (he earned his Ph.D. at the age of twenty-five), Dr. Bettmann has always admired and profited by the entrepreneurial spirit that governs his adopted country. In America, he wryly notes, "success looms if you work with unceasing abandon."

Finally, Bettmann's is the story of a long and unusually productive life that continues to enrich those who come in contact with him as he approaches ninety years of age. While he was still struggling to establish the Archive, Dr. Bettmann began a sideline career as an author that has since yielded a dozen highly regarded books, many of which are still in print. It should come as no surprise to learn that through the years he has engaged faithfully in a daily mental and physical regimen that has enabled him to remain creative and productive long beyond the biblical three-score and ten.

Like a fugue from his beloved Bach, which begins with an initial theme, undergoes increasingly complicated variations and counter-points, then returns surely to its source, here is Otto Bettmann's story—in his own words—with a generous selection of pictures, of course.

My favorite pastime: roaming through *The Bettmann Portable Archive*, a volume that sums up a lifetime of picture research and bookmaking. Photo © 1988 by Michael O'Connor.

1   THE MAKING OF A PICTURE MAN

That books and pictures were to be the mainstays of my life seemed to be forecast by this early photo of "the picture man," age two (right), and his brother Ernst, seven.

HOW DO WE BECOME what we are? One's place of birth is certainly a major factor. I was particularly fortunate to see the light of day and pierce the air with my first scream in Leipzig, on October 15, 1903. Leipzig was a town with a luminescent cultural tradition.

To be born in such an environment is a case of benevolent fortuity. It brings to mind the childhood game of blowing to the four winds the seeds of dandelions, each equipped with a tiny parachute. Some seeds land in a stony field, wither, and die. Others end up on fertile soil to grow and flower.

There are, of course, exceptions to this rule. A child who begins life under adverse conditions may still achieve excellence through guts and initiative. One is reminded of William Dean Howells, the arbiter of American literature in the 1890s and editor of the *Atlantic Monthly,* who educated himself on the rugged Ohio frontier by studying old copies of newspapers with which his father had wallpapered his log cabin (see Howells, *My Year in the Log Cabin,* 1893). But I was fortunate to be set down in a richly nurturing soil. A combination of favorable circumstances shaped my character and launched me on a highly unconventional career.

Centrally located in the German realm, Leipzig had for centuries been the focus of Europe's international book trade. Hence it may be said, with a little poetic license, that I was born amidst the clacking of

Statue of philosopher-mathematician G. W. Leibniz in the courtyard of Leipzig University.

printing presses. (Some friends, knowing of my bookish bent, claim I was born in a library nook, but this is stretching the truth.)

Not only was Leipzig still the uncontested center of the book trade, but the town's intellectual atmosphere was further enhanced by a renowned university—founded in 1409 and later to become my alma mater. One of its most distinguished graduates was Gottfried Wilhelm Leibniz, acknowledged as one of the seventeenth century's leading intellectual geniuses. Leibniz was the developer of integral and differential calculus, anticipating the computer age. I can remember my father showing me the Leibniz monument on the university campus and explaining to me (to little avail, no doubt) the significance of this great man.

More important to us children was not Leibniz the scientist, but Leibniz the man after whom our favorite cookies were named. Leibniz Biscuits were given to us when we were sick, or pretended to be. To this day, one can go to any American supermarket and find Leibniz cookies in the imported baked goods department.

The memory of great men in literature and music reverberated through our town. Johann Wolfgang von Goethe spent three happy years in Leipzig (1765–68) and emerged as one of the world's greatest lyrical poets. He praised Leipzig as his "Little Paris" and commended its citizens on their search for *Bildung* (culture).

Leipzig: a town resounding with the sonorities of Bach.

IF LEIPZIG THE book town exerted an early influence in making me an inveterate bookman, the town's added distinction as a center of music kindled in me a lifelong interest in this "divine art." Johann Sebastian Bach spent twenty-seven years in Leipzig (1723–50) as music director of the Thomas Kirche (St. Thomas Church). It was the period of the master's most miraculous productivity, during which he wrote an endless flow of works that delight us to this day.

Still, Bach's Leipzig years were by no means the happiest of his career. He was forced to engage in frequent, heated disputes with the twenty tin-eared burgomeisters of Leipzig, who were unaware of his genius and persistently denied him funds for his orchestral ventures. "Our incorrigible *kantor*" was their unenlightened assessment of J. S. Bach.

That Bach and his music were impressed so early on my mind was probably due to the location of the house in which I spent much of my youth. In 1909, when I was six years old, my father, a successful orthopedic surgeon, had established a clinic in a five-story building at

View from the balcony of my child-hood home. The Thomas Kirche (left) was Bach's dominion during his Leipzig stay (1723–50) as cantor and music director.

20A Thomas Ring, about five hundred feet from the Thomas Kirche. The third-floor residential quarters had a semicircular balcony that afforded a commanding view of "Bach country," in whose center fate seemed to have set me down.

A more concrete reminder of this musical giant greeted us on the way to school when my brother Ernst and I passed the Thomas churchyard, with the Bach monument at its center. We looked up at the statue in a mood of mystified admiration—vaguely aware of its importance, though not sure why. Leipzig's pigeons weren't quite as respectful. Bach's head was one of their favorite roosts, and it showed.

A pivotal annual event was the Good Friday performance of Bach's *St. Matthew Passion*. Leipzig's music lovers eagerly awaited the concert as a stirring, almost sacramental high point of the year. The sense of anticipation shared even by us youngsters can be easily explained: the blessings of mechanical sound transmission were still decades away. We had to wait all year to hear the *St. Matthew Passion*. How lucky are today's audiophiles, who are able to conjure up any master-work simply by pushing a button.

The most exciting event centering on Leipzig's greatest musician

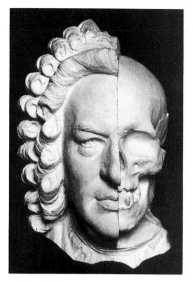

Bach's skull (above), discovered early in the century, was used by the sculptor Karl Seffner as the model for the Bach monument (right) in the courtyard of Leipzig's Thomas Kirche close to the Bettmann home.

was the celebration of New Year's Eve at our home. My parents made a tradition of inviting their friends for a party on this special night. As the midnight hour approached, the guests grabbed their hats and coats and rushed to our balcony facing the Thomas Kirche. The city lay in almost total darkness, but as the church bells chimed twelve, the lights of the church tower came on as if by magic. The tower's top seemed miraculously suspended in midair, and a group of town trumpeters began to intone Bach's gripping chorale:

The year is past, and well may we
to God our Lord most thankful be . . .

It was a staunch and faith-inspiring melody, with succeeding verses a resounding affirmation of the perpetuity of God's grace. This little drama, almost surrealistic to our young eyes, was for us children like a message from heaven—a once-a-year event eagerly anticipated and

Town musicians playing Bach chorales on New Year's Eve from the tower of the Thomas Kirche—an emotion-packed event witnessed each year by the Bettmann family and its circle of friends.

deeply etched on our impressionable minds. It made us "Bachants" for life.

Although the image of Bach is that of a preeminent Christian musician, it is interesting to note that during my youth, in a time of increasing anti-Semitism, Jews participated actively in church performances of this master's works. I myself was recruited at age ten to sing with other Jewish and Christian boys in the Auxiliary Boys Choir, which performed on the second Sunday of each month in the Thomas Kirche. With the openness of children, we saw nothing contradictory in the fact that we went to synagogue on Friday and sang to the glory of Christ on Sunday. Looking back on it now, I can see that we simply enjoyed the music of Bach for what it was—works of extraordinary beauty that provided a rich emotional experience for each of us. We were hardly aware that this sublime music had emerged from religious beliefs quite different from those to which our own families were committed.

The Bettmann family shortly after its move to Leipzig's "Bach country" in 1908: father (Dr. Hans I. Bettmann), Mother (Charlotte), and the boys, Ernst and Otto. Very musical themselves, my parents insisted that we learn to play an instrument.

Early musical training exerts a shaping influence for life.

LIVING IN A highly charged musical atmosphere as we did, it was only natural that my brother and I would take up an instrument. Our father, an enthusiastic cello player, set a good example. Every Wednesday night he joined three other amateur musicians to play Mozart and Haydn quartets. This otherwise harmonious group had its squabbles, some mirroring the mood of deepening anti-Semitism then manifesting itself in Germany.

On one occasion my father proposed that the group tackle some chamber music by Mendelssohn. The violist, Herr Hedrich—a rangy vintner's son of pure Aryan descent from the Rhineland—protested vigorously, sniffing, "Let's not get involved with that sentimental *Juden Musik* [Jew music]."

One can imagine my father's dismay that this fellow musician, whom he otherwise liked, should echo the anti-Semitism that was becoming ever more vocal, even within "polite" German society. But it was hardly a new phenomenon among Germans. Indeed, the epithet *Juden Musik* in reference to the works of Mendelssohn was first employed by the German genius Richard Wagner, a notorious anti-Semite. In our family, we were always aware of this undercurrent of Jew-hatred even among the most civilized of our compatriots, but we had wished to believe that the "Holy Grail" of music was exempt from such disharmonies. In any event, soon after this incident my father's quartet broke up.

My musical training was not without its ups and downs, but it had altogether a character-shaping influence. Starting at the age of six, I studied with Herr Enger, a violinist in the famed Leipzig Gewandhaus Orchestra. As a part-time piano teacher, he was rather lackadaisical in his discipline—letting me play "light classics" one after another, without insisting that I perfect any before proceeding to the next. After three years under his tutelage (or the lack of it), I fancied myself an incipient virtuoso. But Herr Enger did not give me the solid grounding I needed in piano technique.

Sensing that I needed more of a disciplinarian, my parents took me to a reputedly more exacting teacher, appropriately named Fräulein Schütze (two ominous umlauts, a name connoting "sharpshooter"). Meeting her for the first time, I thought it would be a cinch to impress her with a fast-paced little trifle. To my chagrin, when I finished the piece she ripped my playing to pieces. My pride deeply hurt, I nearly drenched the keyboard with tears. I remember my mother asking me, "Otto, do you have a cold?" On our way home, with raised fists I swore I would never accept Fräulein Schütze as my teacher.

RES·SEVERA·VERUM·GAUDIUM.

Motto over the entrance of the Leipzig Gewandhaus: "Only the pursuit of the serious [will give] true pleasure." When we were children, our parents occasionally took us to this famous concert hall, where Felix Mendelssohn first conducted.

My parents were of a different resolve. After the application of parental pressure that included some "corporal convincing," I ultimately gave in. In retrospect, I must admit that I am most grateful to my parents for this bit of unprogressive education.

Fräulein Schütze took me back to the basics: scales, technique, and intensive study of Bach, music's greatest pedagogue. She always insisted that I first gain complete command of the technical aspects of a piece before attempting a musical interpretation. I tackled the simple gavottes, minuets, and marches Bach had written for his young sons, then I progressed to more involved pieces (though I never made it to the *Goldberg Variations,* perhaps piano music's most challenging masterwork). When I was fifteen I became her master student and the star of her annual recitals. She taught me to approach a musical piece methodically and to stick with it until I truly grasped it—principles that shaped the working philosophy that has guided me all my life: master the elemental before tackling the complex.

Perhaps we can distill a drop of applicable truth from my early pianistic experience. The crux of the matter is that, left to themselves, children as a rule will not learn to play an instrument well. Parents have to exert some benevolent pressure in order to bring forth the serious effort and resolve required to buckle down and practice. If parents are able to accomplish this, they will send their children into the world with a precious gift.

In spite of my lifelong devotion to the piano, I will never be an Arthur Rubenstein (admittedly he at times hit wrong notes, but that's the only thing I have in common with him). When I recently asked a fine virtuoso, Judith Burganger (professor of music at Florida Atlantic University), about the state of my piano playing, she said, "You play with laudable fluency—maybe a little too fast and with a little too much pedal—but after listening to you I can vouch for your good heart." This made me rather happy. What else is music for but to bring out what's inside? As one who has reaped so many benefits from the rigors of my early, enforced musical training, I must recommend to all parents to see to it that their children learn to speak this language of the heart—whatever their choice of instrument.

Father's library wakens an early interest in books quaintly illustrated.

Athanasius Kircher, the Jesuit inventor, envisioned the future. His works were the center of my father's book collection.

I MUST GIVE CREDIT to my father for introducing me early in life to the world of books and pictures. His own bibliophilic interests were surely one of the most decisive influences on my career—making books my lifelong love and subtly nudging me toward things pictorial.

My father had become an ardent book collector with a special interest in the works of the seventeenth-century Jesuit scientist Athanasius Kircher (1601–1680), who was born in the Bettmann family's hometown of Geisa. I am sure that pride in his landsman fired my father's enthusiasm for Kircher, who is recognized today as one of the period's most original minds. This scientist, linguist, and inventor had humble beginnings as a Catholic cleric, officiating in various German towns. His career and worldwide fame were established only after he went to Rome in 1633, driven there by the upheaval of the Thirty Years' War.

In Rome, Kircher became a world-renowned linguist, biblical scholar, and acoustic researcher, writing no less than thirty-two heavy and profusely illustrated tomes. In the field of acoustics, he had decidedly prophetic leanings, anticipating among other things sound transmission over long distances—the radio and the telephone. Models of mechanical pianos and slide projectors were among the

A Kircher device to help the hard-of-hearing.

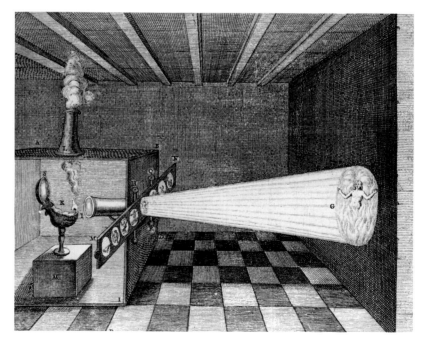

The lantern slide projector envisioned by Kircher is quite sound in design, except that his slides are illuminated by the flame of a primitive oil lamp.

This drawing may be aptly titled "The First Radio Station." It shows Kircher's suggestion for a bugging device enabling the lord of the castle (right) to hear conversations going on in the courtyard (left). The sound channel (center) is modeled after the human ear's cochlea. In 1938, this illustration was used in a CBS advertisement that gave the Bettmann Archive national exposure.

The command horn of Alexander the Great, designed to carry the king's voice over long distances.

Exposure to books and illustrations made me conscious at an early age of the fascination of pictures, which I searched out with juvenile avidity. Apparently, I wasn't the first Otto so afflicted—as shown in the frontispiece of the book *Otto of the Silver Hand* (1888), by Howard Pyle, American graphic artist and writer.

inventions on display in Rome's Museum Kircherianum, which became the nucleus of the famed Vatican Museum. A tireless, inventive dabbler, Kircher has been called "the Thomas Edison of the seventeenth century."

Whenever my father located a new Kircher work, he proudly showed the find to us children. Although we couldn't read Kircher's Latin text, we delighted in the numerous unusual and fascinating illustrations. This early exposure to extraordinary graphics no doubt planted in my mind the seeds that would germinate and steer me—if unconsciously—in the direction of graphic history and, much later, to conjure up the idea of the Bettmann Archive. Indeed, one of the Kircher pictures—that of a prototypical radio station—would resurface at a strategic time early in my American days and help me establish myself in my new profession (see chapter 2).

My father was also responsible for my early fascination with rare books. He was a member of an exclusive bibliophile society called "The Leipzig Ninety-nine"—a circle of book enthusiasts, designers, and printers who annually issued finely designed illustrated books, each in a run of just ninety-nine copies. On the evening of the society's annual meeting, we children were permitted to stay up until Father came home with the bibliophilic harvest of the year—a big bag of fine books and keepsakes. These treasures were inspected by us with cries of wonder and amusement. I still have some of these, among them a miniature book measuring but one inch high, titled *A Guide and Warning to Young Couples About to Marry*. It is a far cry from our Masters and Johnson sex manuals.

THE MAKING OF A PICTURE MAN

Illustration from *The Difficult Assignment*, one of the luxury editions still in my library that the Leipzig bibliophile club printed for its ninety-nine members exclusively.

Another gem issued by the Leipzig Ninety-nine and imprinted with my father's name is titled *The Difficult Assignment* (*Die Schwierige Aufgabe*). It was illustrated by Hans Alexander Müller, who later came to the United States (because his wife was Jewish) and established himself as a leading book illustrator for the Limited Editions Club, Random House, and Doubleday. The book tells of a group of intellectuals in the town of Flachsensingen—"small in size but great in culture." The entrance hall to their club was adorned with the marble statue of a nude Venus. It seems that the sculpture's posterior had become blackened over the years because none of the club's learned visitors ever passed the goddess without giving her a loving pat. The club's high command faced the "difficult assignment" of repairing the damage done to the once-sparkling piece of divine anatomy.

X rays puzzle the young pictorialist.

THE EARLY APPEARANCE of the phenomenon of X rays on my mental screen was another deciding factor in steering me toward the pictorial. In his premedical years in the 1890s, my father had studied at the University of Würzburg with Dr. Wilhelm Roentgen. At the time, this little-known physicist was on the verge of the world-shaking discovery of X rays that later would earn him the Nobel Prize in physics (1901).

On November 8, 1895, Roentgen noted a strange luminescence emanating from a vacuum tube. Unable to explain the phenomenon, he called the radiation "X rays." The new technique of using X rays to reveal the human bone structure took the medical world by storm.

My father's clinic included a Department of Roentgenology, where X-ray pictures were taken, processed, and interpreted. As a young boy I often went to the department's darkroom to watch an assistant develop the eight-by-ten-inch emulsion-covered yellow glass plates. It was here that I had my first heady sniff of developer and fixing baths, an acrid aroma with which I was to become intimately familiar.

The roentgenology department was a source of great pride to my father, and he never tired of talking about it. In those early days there was often trouble with the X-ray tubes, which were still in an infant state of development. A verse my father quoted to my mother, with a deferential smile, still sticks in my mind:

X-ray tubes can be a bust,
And, like women, hard to trust.
Sometimes they are sweet and good.
Then they crackle, sour in mood.

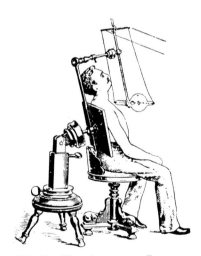

Primitive X-ray instrument. Exposure times averaged ten minutes. Doctors were not yet aware that X rays could cause cancer and life-threatening burns.

BETTMANN

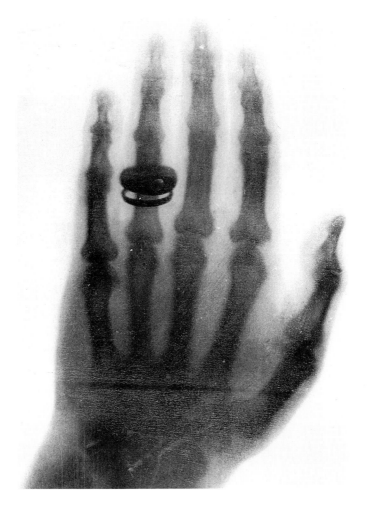

Above: Dr. Wilhelm Roentgen (1845–1923), whose research gave rise to radiology. My father studied with him in the late 1890s at Würzburg University. Right: one of Roentgen's early X-ray photographs, showing the skeletal structure of his wife's left hand. This picture was prominent in my father's X-ray room and was one of my first pictorial impressions. Thousands more were to follow in a long career.

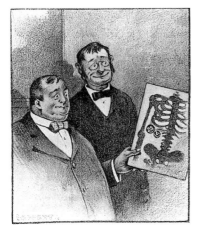

A popular magazine made fun of the new discovery—suggesting that the typical doctor would first X-ray a patient's pocketbook to see if it contained enough money to make an operation financially worthwhile.

In the Bettmann household, an "X-ray frolic" became a main attraction of children's birthday parties. My father took the boy and girl visitors to the X-ray room, where, half frightened and half excited, they could see their own skeleton, a ghostly structure appearing under their flesh. One can imagine little Elsa running home from a Bettmann party and telling her mother breathlessly, "Guess what I saw today? Fritz's heart beating—inside his skeleton."

We now know that X rays are no children's game—or adults', for that matter. X-ray applications have evolved into high technology. Even President Reagan's multibillion-dollar missile defense plan was based on X rays bonded with laser beams.

Another item in the Bettmann X-ray room became symbolic of my budding interest in things pictorial. Displayed on the back wall was a picture of the hand of Dr. Roentgen's wife, showing her wedding ring on a skeletal finger. I think Roentgen himself had given this copy to my father during his Würzburg days. This image was one of the earliest to make a deep impression on me. Reproduced innumerable times since, it can rank as picture number one in the Bettmann

THE MAKING OF A PICTURE MAN

Archive—or at least in the Bettmann consciousness—with many thousands of strange images to follow.

My father's involvement in the experimental era of X rays had a tragic epilogue. Neither Dr. Roentgen nor his disciples could have anticipated the dangerous, tissue-destroying side effects of this wondrous discovery. Now this radiation can be controlled and used as a lifesaving therapy, but among its pioneers it was often the cause of "X-ray cancer," a pernicious destruction of tissue for which there was no known cure. Throughout his life, my father suffered the ill effects of X rays. He heroically faced the affliction, losing one finger after another to amputation. He submitted to many skin transplant operations, none successful, and his X-ray cancer eventually proved to be fatal.

High school: classical training shapes my youthful mind.

IT IS NOT ONLY where and what you learn but also the experience of living with one's young contemporaries that makes high school such a vital influence on one's character.

The school I went to, a humanistic gymnasium, Die König Albert Schule, was slanted toward the linguistic. Latin, Greek, and modern languages dominated the curriculum. We sweated out nine hours a week of Latin and six hours of Greek, besides being subject to a fairly strict regimen of modern French and English.

Knowledge of French and English was a practical necessity in Europe—particularly in Germany, where, assuming you lived in its central part, a trip of two or three hundred miles brought you to the border of another country with its own distinct language. Americans, settled on a vast continent and able to communicate freely with millions of their countrymen, be they in Alaska or Texas, are fortunate to live in a linguistically unified nation.

Considering the classical training I received, one might ask what was the use of learning dead languages. The humanists had a ready answer: classical languages were taught to us not for everyday use but to acquaint us with the great civilizations of the past; to shape our budding minds by exposing us to systems of thought that remain valid to this day.

Quite frankly, I have forgotten much of the Latin and Greek that was drilled into me in high school. Still, even if one forgets the details of subject matter, the discipline acquired in the process—learning how to learn—will prove to be a lifelong benefit, an invaluable asset for any field of endeavor one may enter. A logical grid remains embedded in one's cerebral computer, from which one profits during a lifetime even if few words are retained. As the learned French statesman Édouard Herriot once observed, "Culture is what's left when one has forgotten everything else."

Painful encounter with anti-Semitism instills a will to succeed.

DURING MY HIGH SCHOOL years, along with book learning came the psychological shaping of my attitude toward the world and my fellow citizens with whom I was destined to live. When I was about twelve years old, I had my first traumatic encounter with anti-Semitism.

I was the only Jewish boy in a class of forty and seemed to get along well with my comrades, although they undoubtedly felt some discomfort over my "otherness." This unease remained under control until one day it surfaced just before class was to begin. A rather fresh boy went to the blackboard and wrote: "All Jews are swine. Bettmann is a Jew; hence Bettmann is a swine."

I don't recall the reaction of the class, but I am sure that no voice of protest was raised. This outburst of anti-Semitism against me, a highly sensitive and admittedly insecure youngster, had a crushing effect.

Me at age fourteen, looking somewhat forlornly from the balcony of my father's house. I was a sensitive youth, and anti-Semitic insults in high school gave my character a turn toward the melancholic.

While the *Herr Rector* (headmaster) tried to respond to my mother's outraged complaints with apologies and a severe reprimand of the culprit, the incident left me deeply scarred. It was in fact a turning point in the development of my personality. Once a generally cheerful youngster, I now tended to become far more withdrawn—engaged in inner monologues instead of seeking the companionship of my peers, whom I perceived as being in a hostile camp. It is also possible, however, that this trauma simply brought out in me a latent melancholic streak.

On the positive side, this incident unleashed in me a new sense of determination to better myself and rise above petty discrimination. "I will show these guys that I am not only equal to them, but even superior," I thought. No doubt my early confrontation with anti-Jewish feelings had a determining effect on my later life. Professionally, it made me somewhat overambitious. But it also led me, as a Jew, to feel that I had to be doubly sure to observe the highest ethical standards in my pursuit of success, for I felt that the Gentile world would judge me and my fellow Jews on a more stringent scale. My reaction bears out Freud's observation that being born a Jew in a hostile world can turn into a benefit, offering the opportunity to strengthen one's moral muscle.

If my high school days contributed in an unforeseen way to the development of my inner self, they were also marked by a considerable intake of knowledge. At the end of our tenure we had to pass the *Abiturienten Examen* (*abitio*—"I leave"), a punishing week of oral grilling and paper writing. My assignment consisted of interpreting and commenting on Sophocles' observation from *Antigone:* "Mighty as nature is, there is nothing in nature mightier than man"—no lightweight topic for an eighteen-year-old to tackle.

University studies and "wandering years."

GIVEN MY PREDILECTIONS, I chose cultural history and art as my fields of academic study. There was no problem getting into a college once one passed the *Abiturienten Examen*. A passing mark was the equivalent of a junior college degree, serving as an entrance ticket to academia—no anxious waiting for acceptance letters.

Once enrolled at the University of Leipzig in 1921, I was not faced with the tyranny of testing that prevails and is widely criticized in modern American schools. The system of working for points was alien to us. One had to take certain required courses and get credit for papers and oral presentations. Once the dissertation theme was as-

Entrance to Leipzig University, adjacent to the Pauliner Universitäts Kirche (right) and Leipzig's renowned opera house (far right). The university was bombed by Allied forces during World War II and later replaced by a forty-story skyscraper.

signed, a student was expected to work without professorial supervision.

One may say that ours was an elitist education designed to benefit only the wealthy and the privileged. Higher education in the Western democracies seems to have pursued different aims, opening its doors to the multitudes—a laudable notion, but one with some distinct pitfalls. Some institutions have lost sight of the original purposes of a university—to provide a broad *universal* understanding of life—and have tended to become training programs for business and the professions, with even their advanced degrees serving primarily as passports for better-paying jobs.

In the school I attended, dormitory living was unknown. A student rented a room from someone in town. If he was lucky, it turned out to be a *sturmfreie Bude* (safe pad), where lady visitors could be smuggled in.

Though Germany was notorious for its rampant anti-Semitism, it did not have a *numerus clausus*—that is, German schools did not limit the number of Jewish students they would accept. Strangely enough, democratic America was less tolerant in this respect. As late as 1922, President Lowell of Harvard openly called for his school's participation in a quota system restricting the admission of Jewish students. Dartmouth followed suit, and quota systems remained in effect in some elite American universities until after World War II.

If religion was immaterial and students could advance in German universities unimpaired by discrimination, it was a different story for teachers of the Jewish faith. They might become full professors only in rare instances. However distinguished, many Jewish academicians re-

Paleontology professor Heinrich Finke (above) was a classroom horror during my two semesters at the University of Freiburg. But he taught us much. At right is the cathedral of Freiburg, one of Germany's most graceful and stylistically pure Gothic churches, built between 1122 and 1152. Ascending behind the cathedral's spire are the foothills of the Black Forest mountains—a magic region that we students often visited.

mained *Privatdozenten*, reaching at best the status of "extraordinary professor." The highest rank—"ordinary professor," a title reserved for department heads signifying the acme of academic accomplishment— was an honor rarely bestowed upon a Jew.

An unusual feature of our university life was the way students shifted the locale of their studies from school to school, spending a semester in one university, the next semester at another, at times far away. The practice was reminiscent of the wanderings of the medieval journeyman, who had to move from job to job and town to town before receiving recognition as a master craftsman.

My *Wanderjahre* (wandering years) included two semesters at the University of Freiburg on Germany's southern border. Dominated by one of Germany's great Gothic cathedrals, Freiburg is a scenically beautiful town close to the *Schwarzwald* (Black Forest). My studies there with the famed paleographer Heinrich Finke and the archconservative historian Von Bellow (and bellow he often did) caused me some trepidation. The two professors were much feared for their strictness, and we students trembled going to their seminars. One of my assignments in Professor Finke's class was to interpret a feudal-era Latin document in archaic Carolingian script. I spent nights before the session in study with my friends, rehearsing the translation. When it

Professor Edmund Husserl. As the founder of phenomenology he achieved worldwide fame, but students found his lectures far beyond their comprehension.

came time for my presentation, things went smoothly because I knew the text almost by heart.

Other teachers were more easygoing, and in this department Professor Edmund Husserl took the prize. At lecture time, an absent-minded, goateed Jewish man entered the class, affixed his pince-nez, and began reading in an almost inaudible voice from a prepared text. As he mumbled on, we grasped little, becoming utterly bored. Still, this world-famous scholar—who almost single-handedly developed the philosophy of phenomenology—was to be accorded the proper respect. When he finally took off his pince-nez, signaling the end of his lecture, we greeted him with a salvo of applause in the form of stomping feet (which took the place of clapping hands in German universities). I have often wondered whether this tribute was one of gratitude or extreme relief.

In spite of his failings as a speaker, Husserl has become a major figure in the world of philosophy. In the past few decades he has achieved a status almost equal to that of Immanuel Kant. His studies of phenomenology have had a marked impact, not only on philosophy, but on linguistics, literature, and semiology—practically all fields of learning. But alas, what is the use of denying it? Though I can boast of having studied with Husserl, I am unable to this day to explain in a few clear words what phenomenology really purports to be.

After my year at Freiburg (1926), I returned to the University of Leipzig to complete my doctoral dissertation, *The Emergence of Professional Ethics in the German Book Trade of the Eighteenth Century.* The thesis dealt with the literary pirating common in the eighteenth century and the attempt of publishers to stop the abuse and exert pressure on the government to enact copyright legislation.

First professional job; the amazing Hinrichsen family.

AFTER COMPLETING MY academic studies and getting my Ph.D., I was fortunate to land what seemed an ideal job in Leipzig in 1927. Hooked on books and enamored of music, I couldn't have asked for a better place to work than in a music publishing firm. C. F. Peters had been prominent in this field since the early 1800s (and it remains so to this day).

Since the position was offered to me because of family connections, I had been spared the painful process of hunting for a job. My parents had been friends with the Hinrichsen family for years. Henri Hinrichsen was the sole owner of C. F. Peters, and his remarkable wife, Martha, and my mother were in friendly contact daily. The Bettmann

THE MAKING OF A PICTURE MAN

Joseph Karl Stieler's painting of Beethoven writing the *Missa Solemnis* is recognized as one of the most telling portraits of the master. It hung in the Hinrichsen music room but is now a prized possession of the Beethoven Haus in Bonn.

Envelope of a letter from Beethoven to his publisher, C. F. Peters (1822). The Peters archive contained many priceless manuscripts.

boys had spent many happy hours with the seven Hinrichsen children in their palatial home at Talstrasse 10, where the publishing firm and an affiliated research branch, Music Bibliothek Peters, was located. Henri Hinrichsen was one of Leipzig's most distinguished citizens and much involved in civic causes. In recognition of his generosity, Leipzig University awarded him an honorary doctorate. The city named a street after him and he was appointed *Geheimer Kommerzienrat* (exalted commercial counselor). In a most heart-wrenching turn of fate— one that was all too common in the Nazi era—this man and his wife, of the Jewish faith but German to the core, died ignominiously in a concentration camp in 1943.

The Hinrichsen home resembled a private museum crammed with priceless paintings, among them Joseph Karl Stieler's Beethoven portrait, accepted as the most evocative representation of the master. (It is now in the Beethoven Haus in Bonn.) The walls of the music room had recessed windowed wall cabinets in which original music manuscripts were displayed. Among them were priceless Bach cantatas, some of them fortuitously transferred to the United States before the Hitler storm broke.

Henri Hinrichsen was an accomplished pianist. At times he asked me to join him on a second piano to play a Mozart sonata or concerto. I recall one Sunday when he was pleased with my accompaniment— so much so that he went to one of the wall cabinets, opened it, and took out an original page from Robert Schumann's *Album Blaetter*. "You did pretty well today, Otto," he said. "I want you to have this as a memento." I cherished this valuable original until, facing hard times after coming to America, I was forced to sell it. (Walter Schatzki—a prosperous émigré book and manuscript dealer on Fifty-seventh Street in Manhattan—grabbed it for a pittance.) I long regretted having to give it up.

Of all the tasks assigned to me at Peters, I particularly enjoyed working in the vast archives that stored priceless musical manuscripts ranging from Bach to Richard Strauss—a good training ground for a future archivist. Moreover, my job had attached to it an inviting prospect: I was to be trained for a year in the firm's Leipzig headquarters to learn all aspects of the business, after which, I was promised, I would be sent overseas to develop and head the firm's U.S. branch. This prospect became even more appealing when the Hinrichsens' eldest son, Max, returned from an exploratory trip to the United

Above: Edvard Grieg and his wife Nina (left) were guests of Martha and Henri Hinrichsen in Leipzig in 1906. Right: The Peters emporium at Talstrasse 10 in Leipzig. The ground floor housed the firm's editorial offices. Upper floors accommodated the large Hinrichsen family (seven children) in luxurious style.

States and gave me a glowing report of his experiences there. I was eager to go, but there was a surprise in store for me.

One day out of the blue, after about a year at C. F. Peters, *Kommerzienrat* Hinrichsen called me to his office. I can't deny that I was a bit apprehensive, for he was a man given to treating his employees somewhat imperiously. "You have a lifetime job here at Peters," he began. "But the idea of sending you overseas just won't work. You are not the type to establish a business in the U.S.A. You are well qualified in the editorial field but just not aggressive enough to represent us in America." Whereupon I quit—with what I hoped was appropriate dignity.

The idea of establishing a C. F. Peters office overseas was not abandoned. Once I was out of the running, a more "aggressive" representative was found. Eventually Walter Hinrichsen, Henri's second oldest son, and his wife, Evelyn, built up an impressive C. F. Peters operation in the United States, with branches the world over.

I was not unduly crushed by Dr. Hinrichsen's reneging on his promise to me, because the late 1920s found me restless and ready to move on. This was the high tide of the Weimar Republic, and Berlin was fast becoming the hub of the arts, literature, and theater. It was time to get away from the confinements of Leipzig and the loving but somewhat constricting influence of my family. Therefore, after my resignation from C. F. Peters in the fall of 1928, I decided to move to Berlin, where the action was.

BERLIN UNDER THE Weimar Republic proved an irresistible magnet to me. The sheer multitude of talent in the city defied enumeration. The famed conductor Bruno Walter, himself a prominent Berliner, aptly described the scene in his *Themes and Memoirs*, p. 268: "It was as if all the eminent artistic forces were shining forth once more, imparting to the last festive symposium of the mind a many-hued brilliance before the night of barbarism set in."

More than half a century later, it is difficult to recall the excitement that this creative ferment generated among young people who were involved in the arts. For us, it was a feast of the imagination and the senses. Modernism—the avant-garde—was a vital force in almost every aspect of the arts throughout the Weimar Republic, with Berlin its center. The Bauhaus—a laboratory of modern architecture and design directed by Walter Gropius—moved to Berlin under the leadership of Mies van der Rohe. The new approaches to opera then performed in Berlin are today firmly fixed in American repertory: Alban Berg's *Wozzeck*, Kurt Weill's *Mahagonny*, George Antheil's *Transatlantic*. In Berlin, Arnold Schönberg taught and composed, while his *Erwatung* was performed at the Kroll-Oper under Otto Klemperer. The avant-garde in art was represented by Paul Klee and Wassily Kandinksy, both associated with the Bauhaus. Max Reinhardt, the greatest producer-director of Weimar days, experimented at two Berlin theaters with classics—*Hamlet* and *A Midsummer Night's Dream*. And the pioneering expressionist art of the film, which began with

Above: Bertolt Brecht, dramatist and a fierce anti-Nazi fighter during the days of the Weimar Republic, as painted by Rudolph Schlicter (1928). Right: A 1929 painting by Ernst Ludwig Kirchner shows Berlin's Brandenburg Gate.

BETTMANN

Top left: A new type of emancipated woman emerged in Berlin during the 1930s, as shown in Otto Dix's portrait of Sylvia von Harden, a prominent journalist. Top right: Max Reinhardt excited Berlin and later America by his daring staging of dramatic classics such as Shakespeare's *A Midsummer Night's Dream*. Right: Kurt Weill—who wrote the music for *The Threepenny Opera* (1928)—rehearsing with his wife, Lotte Lenya, who went on to a long stage and film career.

The Cabinet of Dr. Caligari, reached its climax with the filming of Heinrich Mann's novel *The Blue Angel*. In this film an Austrian-born American director, Josef von Sternberg, introduced Marlene Dietrich to the world. American moviegoers might be startled to learn that such great Hollywood writer-directors as Billy Wilder and Fred Zinnemann began as documentary filmmakers in Berlin.

Pre-Hitler days see apogee of avant-garde art, theater, and music.

Josephine Baker, the black Venus, was a top star in Berlin's glittering cabaret circuit.

Right: Oskar Kokoschka's portrait of Arnold Schönberg, atonalism's powerful protagonist who taught at Berlin's Hochschule für Musik. Far right: Kokoschka's *Two Lovers*, the artist and Alma Mahler.

The art of the book flourishes.

LIKE MANY OTHER young people, I carried this enthusiasm for new approaches and modern ideas into my own field of interest, that of printing and books. In this field, "functional typography" was the innovation of the day—applauded by some for its clean design, condemned by others for its stripped-down coldness.

Paul Renner's Futura was then the typeface of choice, the expression of modernity in print. It has since become a basic font in use the world over. I became an enthusiastic adherent of the new school, and met the circle of typographic pioneers headed by Jan Tschichold and Herbert Bayer (later a colleague in the United States). This movement rejected decorative elements and exerted a cleansing influence on book design; its impact is still felt today. Of particular interest to me was the innovative way in which these new designers made photography and textual material work together to communicate ideas.

It was within this Berlin environment, amounting to a cultural explosion, that I made my debut as a bookman. After making some initial contacts with Berlin publishers, I was asked by one of them, Dr. Walter Rothschild, to write the history of his firm, which specialized in works on sociology and jurisprudence. This history appeared in 1929 under the title *Staat und Menschheit (State and Humanity)*. My fee for a year's work was 500 marks—hardly a living. A modest succès d'estime, the book was one of my first forays into authorship, with more to come.

Though I enjoyed Berlin's animated bustle, I cannot say that I took the city by storm. Inspiring as my stay proved to be, financially it was a struggle. A friend back in Leipzig, Dr. Hans Bockwitz, director of the German Book Museum, advised me to prepare myself for a more academic, and thus more secure, position. He suggested that I return to Leipzig and enroll for a degree in master librarianship at the university's prestigious library school. I took his advice. This return to my hometown proved worthwhile. My training in classification systems, reference work, and cataloging led me to a deeper involvement in the history of books and illustrations, giving me a solid footing for my later career as a picture librarian.

It took me just a year to earn the degree of master librarian. Having tasted the excitement of Berlin, I had no desire to stay in Leipzig. My new diploma under my arm, I made haste to return to the town where the arts were in a revolutionary ferment.

THE MAKING OF A PICTURE MAN

Reading wheel devised by Italian engineer Agostino Ramelli (ca. 1531–1610)—one of the first pictures I included in the modest file that was to become the Bettmann Archive. This invention presaged today's tape-based reading machine.

"Day of the Book" generates
idea for a topically arranged
picture collection.

BACK IN BERLIN, I had the good fortune to secure a position well suited to my qualifications and personal preferences. In the late 1920s, Die Staatliche Kunst Bibliothek (the Prussian State Art Library, dissolved during the Nazi regime) was an important resource for Berlin's numerous world-renowned art museums. It served as a central library where custodians of the Kaiser Friedrich Museum, the National Galerie, and other state museums could do their research. At the time I applied for a job, the Kunst Bibliothek had a section that had been unattended for some time for lack of an expert curator: the Griesebach Collection, which offered fine examples of rare illustrated books, including some incunabula (books printed before 1500).

After studying my résumé, the director of the Kunst Bibliothek, Dr. Curt Glaser, seemed pleased to welcome me to his staff. A prominent graphic historian in his own right, Dr. Glaser put me in charge of the Griesebach Collection, which I began to reorganize and catalog. Appended to the rare book collection was a section devoted to Japanese woodcuts, mostly of the erotic variety. It was housed in a series of locked bookcases dubbed "the poison cabinets" (*Giftschränke*). My colleagues would smile sheepishly when they asked for the key to the repository, claiming they had to do some "serious research." It was

Below: The erudite elephant reading in his library—a French eighteenth-century cartoon. Right: Equipped with a book harness, a busy housewife strives for Emersonian culture.

Tolstoy reading by candlelight—a sketch from life by Ilya Repin.

while I was working at the Kunst Bibliothek during 1930–33 that the idea for the Bettmann Archive first dawned on me.

In the days of the Weimar Republic, August 28 was annually celebrated as the "Day of the Book," for this was the birth date of Goethe, the unquestioned paragon of German literature. In 1931, some months before the event, Dr. Glaser asked me to assemble an exhibit with the overall theme "Reading and Books in Graphics and Painting."

To say this assignment was right up my alley would be an understatement. I plunged into the project with a vengeance, assembling miniature paintings, engravings, and woodcuts showing people buying, carrying, creating, and reading books. To add to the dramatic impact, I included items on censorship and book burning. Thus, in my first assignment, I had anticipated the Nazi plague that was soon to descend upon Germany and quench the creative fires ignited in the days of the Weimar Republic, doomed all too soon.

The project also induced me to take a new look at the world of art. Up to then I had thought of art in terms of the artist: Gossaert, Rembrandt, Vermeer, Watteau, Picasso. Now I began to see the topical aspects or subject matter of the works themselves. In short, I began to develop "subject eyes." I assembled for my "Day of the Book" exhibit pictures of saints reading, of Rembrandt's mother leaning over a Bible, and of a court scene by Watteau showing a salon with a reader entertaining the ladies.

To have a memento of the event, I had the display photographed and saved the prints in a well-stuffed cigar box. One day, rummaging through this assemblage, I began to wonder, why confine myself to pictures of books and reading? Why not expand this sampling to include pictures depicting printing, paper making, medicine, transportation—a whole gamut of subjects documented in works of art that would add up to a pictorial history of civilization? The idea fascinated me and I vowed to pursue it, at least as an avocational interest. It was in fact the seed that was to flower in the United States as the Bettmann Archive.

As my work continued at the Kunst Bibliothek, the stacks I supervised often resounded with the click of my Leica. In the course of my work, whenever I ran across a good "subject picture"—be it on salesmanship, windmills, baking, or executions—I snapped it, carefully noting its source. During my travels to Italy, France, and the Scandinavian countries, I added voraciously to my picture file, documenting life as it was.

Little did I know that this material would one day form the basis of a profession that I had in a way invented myself. But before this would come to pass, there were still considerable obstacles in the path ahead.

Ominous signs of the rising Nazi tide: impending disaster for German Jews.

ALTHOUGH I ENJOYED Berlin's artistic ebullience, by the early 1930s Germany resounded with the ominous rumblings of Nazism. The streets of Berlin echoed with the footsteps of strutting Brownshirts. The radio crackled with the dire, gurgling threats of Hitler, the house-painter-turned-demagogue, who had a special, hate-filled way with words and knew how to make them heard. (Did not the führer himself later declare, "Without the loudspeaker we couldn't have conquered Germany"?)

Yet among those opposed to the regime and threatened by its outrages, an undercurrent of hope persisted, the belief that this madness would not, could not last. This notion reached its peak on June 30,

Adolf Hitler: "Without the loud-speaker we couldn't have conquered Germany."

THE MAKING OF A PICTURE MAN

Nazi storm troopers collecting "decadent literature" to be burned at a
public demonstration. Book burnings lighted the skies all over Germany, prompting Franklin D.
Roosevelt to observe, "You can burn
books, but you can't burn ideas."

1934, when, in a veritable bloodbath, Hitler murdered seventy-seven
members of his high command. The most significant victim was Ernst
Röhm, Hitler's friend and comrade-in-arms since the very beginning
of the National Socialist movement.

I remember spending the "Night of the Long Knife" with several
friends, all of us glued to the radio. Paradoxically, as the heinous news
filled the air, the mood of the listeners turned to one of hopefulness. We
all agreed that Hitler was finished. What a foolish miscalculation—
though we were not the only ones to underestimate the madman's
threats. So astute a journalist as Dorothy Thompson had once observed, after a brief interview with the führer, that Hitler was a man of
"startling insignificance" and would never become dictator of Germany.

My circle of German-Jewish bookmen felt particularly outraged
when we heard of Hitler's crusade against literature and art. The Nazi
youth seemed to enjoy with special relish the book burnings staged all
over Germany. The books destroyed were those by Jewish authors and
by all writers of liberal persuasion, such as Erich Maria Remarque,

Bertolt Brecht, and Thomas and Heinrich Mann. In the field of art, works by Cézanne, van Gogh, Gauguin, and Matisse were all banned as "decadent." In music, the work of the Russian composer Stravinsky was considered just as "decadent" as the work of the Austrian Jew Schönberg.

For me personally, the fate of the Kunst Bibliothek, the locus of my work for some two years, was truly shocking. I learned later that the Nazis had sent a fleet of trucks to Prinz Albrechtstrasse and shoveled up the library's priceless possessions like so much garbage, dragging them away to an unknown destination. In a telling bit of absurdity, the Kunst Bibliothek became the headquarters for the secret police, an SS compound, and the scene of endless Nazi brutalities.

As George Steiner so aptly remarked in *From Kant to Heidegger,* "It is in the German sphere that the genius of man would seem to touch the summit . . . but from inside the German world must also spring the ultimate inhumanity, the final experiments of man with his own potentiality for evil."

Fired from my job, I start my own picture library.

Dr. Jacob Rosenberg. Though Jewish, he was at first exempt from Nazi decrees because he was a World War I veteran. He had the unpleasant task of firing me from my position at the Kunst Bibliothek during the first Nazi purge of 1933.

INEVITABLY I WAS CAUGHT in the maelstrom. One of the first acts by Chancellor Hitler in 1933 was to decree that all Jews in *Staatsdienst* (state employment) be fired forthwith. Many fine German officials were forced to discharge their Jewish associates and play the role of hangman.

My case was somewhat different and almost paradoxical: I was fired by one of my Jewish superiors, Dr. Jacob Rosenberg, a world-renowned expert in Dutch painting and curator of the Kaiser Friedrich Museum's Print Cabinet. As a veteran of World War I, he himself was exempt from Hitler's decree—at least temporarily. Like all German officials, when he greeted a "comrade" he was compelled to raise his hand and give the Nazi salute, "Heil Hitler!" People critical of the regime mumbled the words inaudibly and discreetly lowered their right arm toward the lower part of their anatomy. Dr. Rosenberg's tenure as a museum official was short-lived. Soon he too had to leave as the Nazi anti-Jewish rage escalated. First associated with the Fogg Art Museum in Cambridge, he became professor of fine arts at Harvard; he died in 1980.

My enforced unemployment during 1933–34 proved in a way productive. As my father was still able to help me get by, I had the chance to work on a system for my growing picture collection. One of the first things I did was to develop a "visual index": each picture admitted to

THE MAKING OF A PICTURE MAN

My usual Berlin beat—the museum island, with domed entrance to Kaiser Friedrich Museum, one of Europe's richest treasure houses of art.

my file was analyzed as to subject matter, period, and any symbolical application (e.g., a battle scene might be listed under "strategy"; the queen of hearts could be categorized under both "gambling" and "love"). The cross-reference system that evolved permitted the multiple use of each picture while facilitating the speedy tracking down of subjects.

In addition to insisting on careful picture analysis, I also established in my Berlin days another principle that was later to become basic for the Bettmann Archive's expanded operations. Starting from the ground up, I decided to admit to my collection only graphic items of the highest quality—well designed, easily "read," and every inch of them informative. The consistent application of these standards helped the Bettmann Archive become what has been flatteringly called "the Tiffany of picture services."

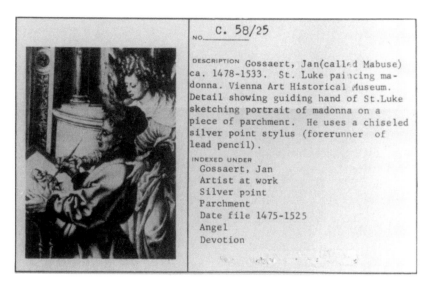

Sample entry from the visual-index system I developed after being dismissed from the Kunst Bibliothek. Each picture was indexed according to artist, subject and date. This facilitated quick retrieval.

At the outset, my visual index filled up a single file drawer. Eventually it would grow into thousands of entries. The picture carrying cards helped the Bettmann Archive achieve a reputation for systematic order and easy accessibility of its resources.

Under the Hitler regime, however, my efforts to earn a living from my picture collection were doomed to failure. Because I had grown up in my father's *Klinik* and was familiar with the medical field, I tried to expand my collection toward medicine in the hope of selling illustrations to pharmaceutical companies that might use such material in ads and mailing pieces. In pursuit of this idea, I made initial contact with Bayer (the aspirin people) and Schering (the medical giant). This merchandising approach met with some initial success: I wrote some articles for the in-house magazine of Hoffmann–La Roche (the pharmaceutical giant) and explored with the Schering people the idea of a medical desk calendar illustrated with old prints. But a new anti-Jewish decree prevented me from continuing on this track.

This law stated that in order to conduct a business, one had to have a license number issued by the Reichshandels Kammer (chamber of commerce). This number had to be displayed on all business communications, including letters, bills, and memoranda. Attempts to

THE MAKING OF A PICTURE MAN

circumvent this law (by employing a straw man, for example) were met with punishment. Of course the Nazis refused to issue a number to any Jewish entrepreneur, even a beginner like me. My attempts to go into business were crushed before I had even begun. The noose was tightening, but as the saying goes, fate has a way of closing one door and opening another—for the lucky ones.

American cousins awaken our interest in that strange land across the sea.

OUR FAMILY HAD the good fortune to have relatives living in the United States with whom we were in continuous and friendly interchange. Not only did my mother, an ardent student of English, correspond regularly with our American cousins, but some of them also visited us every few years in Leipzig. The American Bettmans (our cousins across the seas had dropped one *n* from the family name) were both family minded and very generous. My father, coming from a highly respected but poor branch of the family, could never have become a doctor without the support of these relations. With their support, my father's younger brother, Max, also attended medical school. Max became a staff surgeon in the German navy. A dashing and warmhearted fellow, he resembled in his snappy uniform Prince Heinrich of Prussia, the commander of the German navy.

The guiding spirits of our American relatives were the brothers Alfred and Gilbert Bettman, sons of my grandfather's brother, who had emigrated to the United States in the 1860s. Over the years the family had become prosperous and prominent in Cincinnati and St. Louis and remains so to this day.

Alfred, a graduate of Harvard Law School and a personal friend of the jurist Felix Frankfurter, gained distinction as a town-planning expert. His younger brother, Gilbert, practiced law in Cincinnati, served as vice mayor of that city, and in 1941 was elected justice of the Ohio Supreme Court.

As children, my brother and I were proud of our "uncles from America"—a somewhat mystifying species—and not a little puzzled about that strange continent from which they came. We fancied that all Americans were millionaires, living in skyscrapers. The millionaire idea got stuck in our collective minds when Uncle Levi, one of the first Bettmanns to emigrate, returned to the town of Geisa to join the celebration of my grandfather's eightieth birthday (1912). When the "birthday child" got up one morning he found one of his bathrobe pockets stuffed with a thousand dollars. News of this astounding

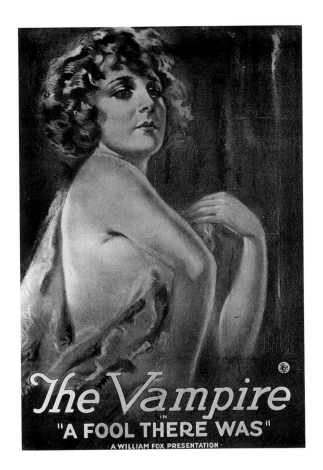

Above: As young children, my brother and I envisioned America as a wild country where knife-wielding Indians still roamed the countryside. Right: We were intrigued by that faraway land—our ideas influenced by early movies which tended to portray American women as flappers and American men as henpecked.

event set the Bettmann hometown aflutter, and the grandchildren caught its reverberation.

When my brother and I were growing up, there still prevailed the idea of the United States as a country with a western tinge where Indians loomed large. This image stuck in our minds because it was the subject of the books accessible to us. We were familiar with Cooper's Leatherstocking Tales. Highly popular too were the novels of Karl May, which gave a vivid picture of the wild and woolly West—notwithstanding the fact that the author had never in his whole life set foot on American soil.

Little known was the vast corpus of American literature dealing with the country's humanitarian strivings, its intensive soul-searching and idealism. Perhaps the names of Thoreau, Emerson, and Whitman rang a bell among the literate. But in general true American culture, its accomplishments in the fields of art and learning, were hardly known. In toto, cultural America had a bad press in Germany. The impending intellectual leadership of the United States became widely known only with the advent of television, which made all the world, in McLuhan's famous phrase, "a global village."

THE MAKING OF A PICTURE MAN

European intellectuals see only the commercial side of the country and mark Americans down as grossly and exclusively money oriented. But regardless of this harsh criticism, the United States has achieved unquestioned leadership in the empire of the mind (art, science, literature), snapping up most of the Nobel Prizes in these fields.

Racing the clock: London meeting with Alfred Bettman, who warns me to leave Germany forthwith.

EVEN AS HITLER'S forward march gained momentum, most middle-class Jews, proud of their *Deutschtum*, continued to delude themselves into thinking that Hitler and the Nazis could not possibly come to power and, once they had, that Hitler "could not last." While the Bettmann family in Germany shared in this false optimism, our American relatives had a clearer perception than we did of the immediate danger we faced as Hitler tightened his hold. We still hoped that the evil storm would blow over, but our American cousins foresaw the bitter end of the Jews in Germany and recognized the dire emergency of our plight.

I was chosen to lead the family exodus, thanks to a personal interest that my cousin Alfred Bettman had taken in my future. (My brother came to the United States in 1938; my parents joined us in 1939.) He invited me to London in the summer of 1934 to discuss the possibility of my emigration to the United States. But Alfred and his charming wife, Lillian, had some persuading to do (testifying to my poor foresight and lack of realism). After all the abuse I had endured, I was still caught up in what was called the German *Kultur-Kreis* (the wholeness and alleged superiority of German culture). My entire nature, my cultural outlook, had been shaped by the society in which I had grown up—leaving it seemed an absurdity. How could I ever hope to survive in what we Germans regarded as the crassly commercial environment of America? But Alfred convinced me I had to leave Germany or face certain doom. In retrospect, I am still shocked at my folly in resisting his importunings. How fortunate I was that I at last yielded to both the logic of his arguments and the fervor of his concern for my family's survival.

Nevertheless, I continued to fret about the possibilities of making a living in the United States. I broached to Alfred the idea of a picture archive along the lines of the one I had tried to develop after losing my government job. He was cool to the notion and instead suggested (judging my character quite astutely) that I should try to make connections with a library or pursue some appropriate post in the aca-

Alfred Bettman, my father's cousin, was a distinguished Cincinnati lawyer and town planner. It was to him that my family owed our survival from Nazi terror.

Left: Alfred and Lillian Bettman at the time of our meeting in London. Without their urging, I probably would have stayed in Germany, facing calamity. Right: London's Big Ben ready to strike an ominous twelve o'clock. With Hitler gaining power, time was running out for me.

demic field. However, he promised to support me if need be during my first year in the United States, whatever career I might choose.

As for Lillian, she rather quickly put me down as not quite the type to succeed in America, objecting in particular to my shy and decidedly European gentility. Once when I hastened to light her cigarette she twitted, "Oh, Otto, you are so Victorian." I guess this was a hint that I was in for quite a culture shock when I did make my move.

Returning to Berlin from my fateful visit to London, I prepared for the break. With thousands of Jews besieging the U.S. consulate, it took almost a year to get my visa—an agonizing wait. And the prospective departure from my friends, the places and things I loved most, and my familiar ways of life weighed heavily on my mind.

THE MAKING OF A PICTURE MAN

Last days in Berlin.

Elisabeth Gergely, my Berlin girlfriend. Though saddened by my imminent departure, she predicted with a fine instinct that I would start a new and happy life in America.

Greek augur predicting the future from the flight of birds.

BERLIN IN THE 1930s was a highly liberated city in matters of sex, outdoing even the sexual revolution of the 1960s and 1970s. Women seemed to have lost all their coyness and innocence. A joke was told of a typical Berliner flaneur who accosted a lady of the street, saying, "Would you like to have a cup of coffee with me—*before?*" Bertolt Brecht and Kurt Weill's *Threepenny Opera,* with its searing erotic songs, was all the rage. The Kurfürstendamm, West Berlin's principal boulevard, had become one of the great pleasure centers of the world, as Berlin developed the decadent nightlife recalled in the film *Cabaret.*

In this ambience of fast-lane living, I was fortunate to find and maintain a friendship with a woman outstanding in character and artistic sensitivity. Elisabeth Gergely—Ergi to her friends—was a goldsmith and jewelry designer trained at the Berlin Kunst Akademie. We met at one of the school's social events, and our friendship lasted for seven years. An immigrant from Hungary, she was divorced from Sandor Gergely, a handsome and gifted photographer and a womanizer *sans pareil.* She lived in a studio apartment in Berlin-Wilmersdorf, one of the city's outlying districts. Though functionally furnished in keeping with the current style, it exuded much charm. The large studio windows opened to a panorama of the rooftops of Berlin.

Ergi was seven years my senior. She was small and slim. Her bohemian setting was somewhat deceiving. Ergi had a very orderly mind, and I, a young man in turmoil, greatly profited from her rational and balanced view of the world. As the time of my departure approached, in late 1935, our conversations took on an air of melancholia. We had ruled out marriage, owing to my uncertain state. (Ergi would eventually flee to Yugoslavia, where she lived out the war in hiding.)

One Sunday afternoon as we sat mooning, something rather unexpected happened. A stray canary flew into the studio through the open skylight. Ergi, a bird fancier, caught it and put it in a cage of artistic design, part of her decor. Being inclined toward the mystic—and aware of the way Roman augurs predicted the future from the flight of birds—Ergi burst out, half crying and half laughing: "You will have a happy landing in America. The bird has found a new home, and so will you." Somehow this prediction gave me a good feeling. It was just one of those irrational, or perhaps suprarational, prophecies that through fate's strange workings finds fulfillment.

Doleful departure.

THE DAY BEFORE I left Germany, my "Aryan" friends and fellow Jews—less lucky than I—gathered to bid me farewell. One of them composed a poem whose first stanza has stayed with me all these years:

Im Begriff sich aufzumachen
Von den scheinbaren Indianern
zu den wahren, ist dem Otto nicht zum lachen.

About to depart
from the apparent Indians [Nazis] to the true ones [American Indians]
Otto doesn't feel like laughing.

I had tried to attend to all the complex formalities that would ensure my smooth departure, but there remained a nagging worry: how would I get clearance to get my picture-crammed steamer trunks across the German–Dutch border? I had booked passage on the Dutch steamer S.S. *Staatendam,* departing from Rotterdam on November 3, 1935, and any delay would be disastrous.

When the critical moment arrived on November 1, the German border guard looked at my bulging luggage rather apprehensively. Befuddled, he asked one of his colleagues to take a look. The two men discussed the situation, and I was able to pick out the phrase *"ein bischen verrückt"* ("some kind of nut"). No doubt they were commenting on what an absurd idea it was to take all those musty old pictures to America. With a somewhat pitying glance, the guard waived me through with, *"Ja, ja, sie können gehen"* ("Yes, yes, you can go").

Sighing with relief, I savored the magic words, feeling like Dostoyevsky in front of the firing squad, reprieved five minutes before his execution (December 22, 1849). Of course, Dostoyevsky then faced four years of servitude in Siberia. In contrast, I was sentenced to paradise.

Strangely—and counter to my expectations—this was to be the last time I would set foot on German soil. This may suggest that I am a vindictive person, which in the testimony of my friends I don't seem to be. But instinctually I cannot forget the Nazi nightmare. The democratic Federal Republic of Germany has tried to make genuine amends—for some thirty years, I have received punctually on the first of each month a small old-age pension from Berlin. Still, my grudge persists. I had in my younger days a good dose of anti-Semitism—hence its antidote, anti-Teutonism, hasn't totally vanished from my

The camera catches me in a pensive mood before my departure. Despite all the abuses I had endured, I did not cherish the idea of leaving my true "fatherland."

THE MAKING OF A PICTURE MAN

system. I have never felt moved during my European travels to visit Germany again. As has been observed, unlike a car, life doesn't come equipped with a reverse gear. The Germans asked me to leave and not very politely—and leave I did, for good.

The passengers on the S.S. *Staatendam* were mostly fellow émigrés, and among this group a mood of apprehension prevailed about the ordeal of adjustment we would be facing. Everybody had some ideas—most of them wrong, based on hearsay. Would we have to run to the police and register? (This was a regulation strictly enforced in the fatherland.) We had heard that American women were a sassy, aggressive species. Some claimed we should be aware of breach-of-promise suits. Stories about rampant Chicago gangs made us fretful that we faced danger from the moment we landed. We thought we would have to do without frankfurters—named after "our" city of Frankfurt. (We were relieved to find, upon our first excursion to an American baseball game, that we would not have to subsist without this popular German morsel.)

Mixed feelings of a reluctant emigrant.

FOR MOST ÉMIGRÉS, leaving one's native land seems like the end of the world. But for me, even though I was still beholden to German *Kultur,* emigration proved in the end to be a piece of good luck. Actually, once I had made up my mind to leave Germany, I looked forward to what I fancied would be a process of renewal or revitalization. After thirty-two years in a country I thought was my own, I was fortunate enough to find the beginning of a new life in the United States. I had the advantage of bringing with me certain cultural and genetic elements that were raised to a higher potency when exposed to the dynamics of American life. Thus, what I brought to my new homeland and what I found there became merged into a new existence, much richer and more exciting than one I could ever have led in Germany.

Americans rarely comprehend their enormous advantage of living and working on a continent that is united linguistically, fiscally, and commercially. The spatially and culturally limited nations of Europe simply don't offer the elbowroom required for personal and professional growth. Immersion in American life allows the narrow view of expatriates from small European countries to expand into an inspiring continental vista. No wonder the multitudes knock at our door.

In receiving these expatriates, America itself was enriched—its own culture expanded and enlarged by the talents of those for whom the

Nazis had only disdain. As Peter Gay (himself a most distinguished emigrant scholar) has noted in *Weimar Culture: The Outsider as Insider* (Torch ed., p. 145), "the Nazi onslaught sent a great many of Weimar Germany's intellectual elite to the death camps and drove many others to desperate acts of self-destruction: But others took the spirit of Weimar into life, into great careers and lasting influence in laboratories, in hospitals, in journalism, in theatres, in universities, and gave that spirit its true home, in exile." I was one of the lucky ones—being spared the languishments of homesickness and jumping into the American melting pot with a sense of joy and liberation.

2  COMING TO

AMERICA:

FREE AT LAST

I SAILED TO America in November 1935 with a pittance in my pocket. The Nazis had seized the meager fund of deutsche marks I had been able to accumulate. They called it a *Reichsflucht Steuer,* a punitive tax for fleeing the Reich. What utter nonsense! I didn't flee of my own volition. They punished me for being chased out.

Though my mood was hopeful, there were some questions gnawing at my mind. What would happen to me in this new, gigantic land? More immediately, where would I go when we landed? Would I have to spend the night on Ellis Island? I had heard horror stories about this place, actually a splendiferous monument to hope that fortunately has been recently resurrected.

After a five-day voyage—uneventful on the whole—I woke up early on November 8. It was still pitch-dark outside. I looked through the porthole, and suddenly a beam of light illumined the waves—no doubt a signal from the Montauk lighthouse. I was strangely touched. Safe at last, I thought to myself. Soon distant lights began to flicker, which to my overwrought mind was a benevolent and hopeful sign. "Things will work out," the ego seemed to assert to the id (or the other way around). As the brisk, clear morning dawned, the ship passed the Statue of Liberty. Everyone rushed on deck and stood transfixed—as if offering a silent prayer.

A group of Russian Jewish immigrants sail into New York harbor, welcomed by the Statue of Liberty. The joy of freedom seems mingled with apprehension over their future in this strange new land.

My apprehensions vanished soon after the ship had docked. I was called to the purser's office and handed a letter from Alfred Bettman, my savior and sponsor. Enclosed was a check for two hundred dollars—"just to get you started," Alfred wrote. The letter ended with the simple but meaning-charged words: "I welcome you to America, and I hope you will like it." As it turned out, Alfred's hopes were not disappointed.

Equally heartening was the fact that my luggage with my picture files was passed through customs without a hitch. A customs inspector, obviously of German descent and with some knowledge of art, glanced thoughtfully through my dossier. I feared rejection for some unforeseen "irregularity," but then the officer smiled at me and said: "You seem quite an art expert. *Dürer nicht wahr?* I am glad you came here. We need people like you." A one-hundred-member brass band could not have given me a more heartwarming welcome.

As I came down the gangplank, the sun shining overhead, I was warmly greeted by a scholarly friend of mine, Julius Held. In his earlier days, Julian, as we then called him, had worked with me at the Kunst Bibliothek in Berlin. He went on to become a world authority on Dutch and Flemish art. His monumental *Oil Sketches by Rubens* was published by Princeton University Press.

Julian had arrived in the United States six months before me. Already well connected with New York University's Institute of Fine Arts, he had the air of a seasoned native. Without further ado, he took me to his residence—a railroad apartment at 20 East Ninety-sixth Street, right off Fifth Avenue. Today this is an area decidedly reserved for the upper crust, but back then the brownstone building, like the neighborhood itself, was in a somewhat dilapidated state. Hence rents were cheap, making it an ideal habitat for newcomers, most of them in the class of the "dignified poor." I was given an eight-by-ten foot garret room at the bargain rate of five dollars a week. My room had a closet without a key, and here I stored the few belongings I had been able to bring with me in the way of photographic equipment and picture material.

My American host and I went out to have lunch in a nearby cafeteria. Assembly-line dining was a new experience for me but one that I developed into a habit in my lean early days. When we returned to my cubbyhole, I was shocked to discover that my two Leicas were gone. Luckily, the boxes of old pictures had been left behind, no doubt judged by the thieves as so much old trash. I later learned that our house, a haven for refugees, was watched by crooks who found the newcomers easy prey.

Julian and I rushed to the police station on Lexington Avenue to tell our tale of woe. Receiving faint sympathy, Julian was prompted to remark, "You can't expect to get action in New York unless there's been a murder." I wasn't exactly encouraged by this revelation, but there was nothing we could do but tramp back to our brownstone. My new life had begun!

An enclave of German refugees. A NUMBER OF immigrant families had taken up lodgings at the brownstone where I lived. It was a lively group of intellectuals, yet I noticed that a downbeat mood pervaded among them. Most of my fellow refugees couldn't quite free themselves from a self-pitying nostalgia. They would frequently hark back to the past, recalling former glories and how beautiful, how cultured (*kultiviert*) things had been in Germany. Once freed, Jews who had been confined for centuries in ghettos and barred from the mainstream of German culture had such an overwhelming desire to prove their Germanness (*Deutschtum*) that it made them apt to become super-Germans (*Alldeutsche*). Having struggled so hard to achieve this *kultivierte* status, such German Jews were naturally reluctant to discard their elitist point of view and too often were inclined to be uppity and arrogant when confronted with run-of-the-mill American culture—so totally different in its roots, so decidedly oriented toward the practical. My fellow expatriates seemed to forget that the same Germany for which they yearned had given them the boot and was doing far worse to those who had remained behind. As for me, although nostalgia was to provide much of my future livelihood, I rarely looked backwards. I was far too excited at having landed in a place so full of miracles and fast action.

I arrived in America in the midst of the Great Depression. I must admit that I was scarcely aware of the hardship and anguish my new countrymen were then enduring. For me, the real depression was in the Germany I had left behind. The United States, in comparison, was clearly a land of plenty. Soon I was even able to send modest care packages to my far more deprived family back home.

English for foreigners.

ONE OF THE most perplexing problems facing many newcomers to the United States is achieving a smooth command of the English language. The better one's understanding of this country's linguistic subtleties, the better one's prospects for success. I had a fairly good background in English, and by the time I reached America I was confident I had the language problem licked. But my immigrant friends begged to differ. They were quick to point out my poor *w*'s (never to be conquered), convoluted sentences, and the Germanic guttural gurgling that marred my attempts to speak like a native.

Stung by this criticism, I made a beeline to City College to register for the course "English for Foreigners." A benevolent Miss Reed tried to introduce a class of about twenty hopeful new arrivals to the secrets of colloquial English. In retrospect, our motley crowd must have resembled what Leo Rosten so hilariously described in the *New Yorker* in his "H*y*m*a*n K*a*p*l*a*n" stories about night school education for immigrants. Miss Reed's final admonition sticks in my mind: "Class, whatever you have learned here, remember that whenever you are asked 'How long are you in America?' be sure to answer, 'I *have been* in America . . .'"

Mark Twain humorously described the speech patterns of my native land as "clumps of succulent Germanic blast." Having been nurtured in the complicated sentence structure of the German language, I always had a desire to master the simple eloquence of English and to add to my word-hoard its succinct and pungent colloquialisms (as in those crisp admonitions "Get lost," "Wise up," and "Get with it," for example). My love affair with English words and phrases led to a hobby of mine that helped me achieve a deeper understanding of my adopted tongue. Since my early days in this country (I am here now fifty-odd years, pardon me, Miss Reed, wherever you are), I have kept copious notebooks I call my "word banks," which list unusually descriptive words and cleverly furbished sayings—the kind that makes one sigh with envy, "I wish I'd written that."

Maybe I should myself heed some of these pearls of wisdom, like Stendhal's observation: "Nobody should try to write what he himself doesn't truly wish to read."

Altogether after so many years granted me in this country, I now feel considerably more comfortable with English than with German. To conquer the subtleties of my new mother tongue I still find endlessly fascinating. Yet my accent and slightly skewed sentence structure I haven't been able to lose. I just have to open my mouth and someone is apt to pop up, "What part of Germany do you come from?" Though I think totally in English, I caught myself, while recently preparing my income tax, doing the addition in a whispered German—just as when I had learned adding in elementary school over eighty years ago. Strange are the ways of the cerebral computer.

My first Thanksgiving, celebrated with Alfred Eisenstaedt.

MY FIRST THANKSGIVING in America was modest—but reassuring in a way. Leon Daniels, a fellow refugee whom I had known in Berlin as manager of the Associated Press, offered to celebrate with me. He brought a friend along. My eyes lit up when Leon introduced him as Alfred Eisenstaedt, already well known in Europe and soon to become one of *Life*'s leading photographers.

Although Eisenstaedt had become a professional photographer rather late (he had sold his first picture when he was twenty-nine), he established himself quickly as a master of the photo essay. One of his most memorable achievements occurred in 1935, when he traveled to Ethiopia and produced a classic photo essay on Emperor Haile Selassie. Eisenstaedt—who would settle permanently in the United States the following year—welcomed me warmly as a newcomer in a field related to his. Leon Daniels, like myself, was to become the founder of a picture agency. His agency, Pix, represented many of the leading émigré photo reporters. Of course, on that Thanksgiving Day we didn't know that we were to plow neighboring furrows.

When Eisenstaedt and I met up with each other at a 1991 exhibit of his photos in Palm Beach, Florida, we reminisced about our meeting long ago in depression-era New York.

In the interest of frugality (which I perhaps had to observe more strictly than my two thoughtful companions), we settled on Thanksgiving dinner at the Horn and Hardart Automat on East Fifty-ninth Street. Horn and Hardart was a chain of self-serve cafeterias where gleaming chrome and glass machines dispensed tasty coffee for five cents and sandwiches and desserts were purchased from little glass cubicles by putting a few coins in a slot. "The Maxime's of the disenfranchised," the playwright Neil Simon called it later on.

After dinner we walked across the Queensboro Bridge and admired the lights of Manhattan. They seemed to have a consoling and welcoming quality, and I gave thanks to the fate that had carried me to these hospitable shores.

Exploring New York and its wonderful libraries.

IN THE NEXT few days, while trying to get the feel of New York, I made some surprising discoveries. Always a book hawk and library browser, I made the rounds of the various city libraries and was much impressed by their facilities and service. In Germany long ago, it was said that librarians deemed themselves "guardians" of books, fearful of having them actually touched by ordinary human hands. I remember trying to borrow a book from Leipzig's municipal library when I was about twelve years old. Filling my simple request involved endless red tape. "Get us testimonials from three citizens," I was told. "Give us a few days, and we will see what we can do." Even at the Preussische Staatsbibliothek in Berlin, we filed our order slips in the morning and were lucky to get the desired books the next afternoon. Taking a book home was out of the question!

In the United States, I discovered that the librarians made every effort to get books into circulation. A European newcomer cannot help but be impressed by the prevailing liberality with which books can be checked out: the open shelves mirror the country's open mind and open society. To this day, I am touched when I see a young mother in a public library checking out a whole batch of children's books for bedside reading or just for thumbing through. This is a privilege totally unthinkable to German "mamas" of my generation.

After living for some three months at the brownstone near Fifth Avenue, I decided it was time to rev up and somehow try to make a living. I had my old pictures—why not try to peddle them around? The prospects weren't the brightest. Who could possibly want such old stuff in fast-growing, forward-looking America? One man to whom I outlined my career plan suggested that I dump my pictures

After a modest Thanksgiving dinner, I took a walk over the Queensboro Bridge with Leon Daniels and Alfred Eisenstaedt, taking in the flickering lights of the megalopolis that was to become our new home—a somewhat emotion-filled experience.

into the Hudson and go back to librarianship. But I wasn't one to be easily discouraged. "Send me some shoes with indestructible heels that I can use for my endless rounds," I wrote to my parents, who had inquired how they could best help me get settled.

My determination to start a business—in the midst of a depression no less—still remains a bit of a mystery to me. As so many of my acquaintances pointed out at the time, my nature and my training were decidedly oriented toward the academic. But it seems I also had been endowed with a modicum of the entrepreneurial spirit. (Maybe my genes had something to do with it. My father, a small-town doctor, had gone to the big city of Leipzig and had ventured to set up his own clinic, Dr. Bettmann's Orthopedic Institute.) As time went on, I even learned to enjoy the rough-and-tumble of the marketplace.

TO ESTABLISH A BASE for my new enterprise, I rented a one-room apartment on West Forty-fourth Street, less than a block from Times Square. This location seemed inviting because a good friend of mine, Paul Jolowicz, a bookseller from Germany, had his office in the same building. But what a devilish place it turned out to be! The building was located directly across from the midtown bus terminal, which announced its presence in high decibels and a battery of neon lights that flashed incessantly at night. It was the ideal resting place for an insomniac like me.

On New Year's Eve, all hell broke loose. Hearing the roar of the Broadway crowd, I couldn't help stepping out at midnight to watch the lighted ball of the New York Times Tower descend to the noise of a sonic explosion. Instinctively, my thoughts harked back to the New Year's celebrations in Leipzig with the melodious Bach chorales—a lyrical, inner-directed evocation, as opposed to the unrestrained outburst of a free and frolicking populace. The contrast didn't discourage me. It was simply a reminder that I was now playing in a totally different ballpark.

By professional standards, the working setup that I was able to put together in my rather cramped new quarters was antediluvian. The clothes closet had to accommodate my enlarger and serve as a makeshift darkroom. Copies had to be rinsed in the bathtub. Metal sheets, used to gloss up paper prints, covered the floor.

My apartment/photo lab was located above the then famous Blue Ribbon Restaurant, renowned for sauerbraten, with Pilsner and Löwenbrau flowing freely. The aromas were particularly tantalizing during those early days when my lunch often consisted of a peanut butter sandwich and a cup of coffee. In contrast, the Blue Ribbon was a favorite hangout of prosperous Germans, among them the famed *Helden Tenor,* Lauritz Melchior.

My friends and I often "dined" in a nearby Chinese restaurant, because there we could get a dish of chop suey for twenty-five cents, and the tea was free. Only on special occasions did we splurge and go to Hector's Cafeteria on Broadway for a full-course dinner at ninety cents. Admittedly, we weren't quite ready for 21 (then the fanciest restaurant in New York).

Nothing, but nothing, happened during my first three weeks of trying to sell pictures. But the beginning of the fourth week brought what seemed to me a true bonanza. I ran across an advertising man who was looking for some pictures of early chemical laboratories, and I was able to produce just what he wanted from my collection. My

Left and center: My modest abode on West Forty-fourth Street, one block from the hustle and bustle of Times Square. While Jews who were chased from Germany had to leave their money behind, they were still permitted in 1935 to take along some household goods. This enabled me to salvage my grand piano and some personal belongings. Right: Fellow immigrants and friends, gathered in my apartment, peruse my photo collection. Happily, all five of the newcomers shown here established themselves well in America. Dr. Eric Proskauer (seated, left) founded Inter Science, a publishing house now part of the John Wiley Company. Standing, left to right, are Hans Alexander Mueller, a Leipzig graphic artist who became a well-known illustrator for American publishing houses; my brother, Ernst, who established a fine medical practice in White Plains, New York; and myself. Rudolf Littauer (seated next to me) became a successful corporation lawyer.

rental fee for these pictures was fifteen dollars, a bargain price if ever there was one, dictated by fear of losing my first sale.

No matter, I was elated; so much so that I decided this was the occasion to partake of the Blue Ribbon's sauerbraten and drink its good German beer rather than just sit upstairs savoring the aromas from below. I invited three of my closest friends in New York to help me celebrate. It was a jolly meal and the check came close to the sale's total. Who cared! This celebration was just what I needed for my morale.

What happened then? I think even O. Henry would have rejected the corny ending of this story. The next day a messenger returned the pictures with a polite note from my customer saying that they were wonderful but didn't quite fit in with a change in plans made by one of the company's vice presidents; therefore, the prompt dispatch of a refund check would be appreciated. In later years, even after the Bettmann Archive had become a fixture in American advertising and publishing, the smell of sauerbraten would still depress me. And I never really quite trusted advertising vice presidents again.

There were other cold-water showers in store for me. Dr. M. F. Agha was then the powerful art director of *Vogue* magazine. Somehow I was unexpectedly ushered into his office in the Graybar Building. He seemed to perceive from my imploring mumblings that I was some sort of a photographer. "We got plenty of photographers," he imperiously declared. "What we need here in America are specialists! Try to concentrate on one subject—like dogs, so I can put you under 'dogs' in my index." A fitting category for me—I left the mighty Dr. Agha

feeling like a dog with its tail between its legs, ready for a good dose of psychotherapy.

After that first disappointment, an unexpected but valuable tip from one of my fellow immigrants gave me new hope. He told me about a veritable clearinghouse to help newcomers to the United States. The Composing Room, a highly regarded typesetting establishment, was headed by Dr. Robert Leslie (who lived to be one hundred and three). He had no equal in befriending immigrants with a graphic arts background. This spirited gentleman, originally a physician, listened to my story. He concluded that my plan of a picture service had fairly bright prospects—"if you plug persistently enough," he added as an afterthought. He also gave me some sage advice: "Be sure not just to call on people as a 'job seeker'—there are thousands of them around—but present yourself as one who has something specific to offer, a man with an identity. Give your picture collection a name."

I invent a new profession: the "backward photographer."

I RACKED MY BRAIN, hoping to come up with a catchy name for my budding business. Bettmann's "The Past in Pictures" was descriptive but too clumsy. "Historic Picture Emporium" seemed too pompous; "Panorama Pictures" too nebulous.

Unable to solve the name problem, which was compounded by my limited grasp of English, I turned to my American friend Paul Standard for advice. Paul was a fine calligrapher and highly literate. His wife, Stella, wrote cookbooks and generously prepared gourmet dinners for the circle of refugees she had befriended in the city. I explained to Paul that my work was in essence that of a photographer who aimed his lens toward the past to reveal a panorama of life as it used to be. In a brilliant flash of inspiration I asked him, "How about printing up a business card with the slogan 'Otto Bettmann, The Backward Photographer'?" You can well imagine how my friend started to laugh. But it was Paul, I believe, who hit on the name "Archive"—an accumulation of ancient documents, preserved and made accessible for research.

The resonance of the word *archive* appealed to me. I later found out that in English the word is commonly used in the plural form, *archives*. I decided to stick with *archive* anyway, because it reminded me of the German form, *Archiv*. Moreover, *archive* conjures up the image of an age-old, state-sponsored institution, to be entered with a proper air of reverence through guarded bronze doors. As a name for my

The artist Friedrich Salloch, a fellow refugee, designed this logo for my struggling enterprise.

business, it is decidedly more appropriate than "The Backward Photographer," and indeed it has served my purpose well.

This image of "ancientness" and venerability often provokes visitors meeting me for the first time to remark, "I thought the Bettmann Archive was founded well over a century ago—yet you're still around?" I am not at all displeased by this reaction; indeed, I feel complimented. People also tended to believe that the Bettmann Archive sprawled over a whole building at least—maybe even a whole city block. In fact, the collection was highly compact and organized rather than a massive, random accumulation of pictures. Only the cream of the crop made it into the Bettmann Archive—all "pictorial meat," as a visitor once remarked.

Dr. Leslie, friend of the immigrants, not only suggested that I find an evocative name for the collection but also provided the initial push that got me started. He introduced me to Percey Seitlin, the editor of his in-house magazine *P.M.* (for "Production Manager"). Percey and I became fast friends, and in his magazine he wrote a little article about me and my work. I still remember its ending: "Bettmann's idea of establishing a picture collection to bid fair to that of our venerable institutions, the Metropolitan Museum and the Library of Congress, is rather overambitious. It seems like starting one's own postal service or railroad system. Well, let him try."

An important figure in the publishing industry evidently had read this article. To my surprise and delight, I received a call from the office of Max Lincoln Schuster, cofounder of Simon and Schuster, asking for an appointment. I made haste to polish up my humble establishment and awaited the great day.

Meeting some of the greats of American publishing.

MAX LINCOLN SCHUSTER arrived at my Forty-fourth Street apartment with an associate, Leon Shimkin. These two men functioned as a highly creative team. Both seemed fascinated with my sundry accumulation of photos, pictorial curiosities, and books. Schuster had an astute "card-index mind." He gathered information from disparate sources, prepared summaries that he called "E.M.'s" (editorial memos), and kept this information accessible in drawers full of reference cards. Time and again during his inspection of my collection he called out to his associate: "Shimkin, look at this. . . . Make a note of it."

Harry Scherman, cofounder and longtime president of the Book-of-the-Month Club, starting a new era in the field of publishing.

Harry Abrams, when he was advertising manager of the Book-of-the-Month Club. He later founded the world-renowned publishing house that bears his name.

Leon Shimkin was to become a major innovator in the mass marketing of books. He founded Pocket Books and Golden Books, both of which revolutionized American publishing. He also popularized Dale Carnegie's books on self-improvement and J. K. Lasser's tax guides. Shimkin eventually took over ownership of Simon and Schuster, creating a greatly expanded publishing conglomerate long before America's merger boom.

As it happened, Shimkin called me a few weeks after his visit to the incipient Bettmann Archive with a request: "Please send over a volume of your *Propylaen Weltgeschichte*—I took a note about it when I saw you. Now Mr. Schuster wants one of his forthcoming books bound in the same material." E.M.'s did for Schuster what computers do for busy managers today—provide an auxiliary memory.

Monetarily, this initial contact didn't bear any fruit, but later on I was to work closely with Simon and Schuster on the illustrations for Will and Ariel Durant's twelve-volume series *The Story of Civilization,* which won a Pulitzer Prize. Also, after our visit Schuster sent me a copy of *Eyes on the World,* one of the earliest picture histories and a book that he himself had edited. He had inscribed it: "With warm good wishes from one picture historian to another." A good omen.

During our first meeting, Schuster called his friend Harry Scherman, one of the founders of the Book-of-the-Month Club, and told him of the picture collector he had encountered. Scherman apparently told Schuster that he would like to meet me, so I paid a call on him at his office.

Harry Scherman was the epitome of a bookman—slightly built with a chiseled face. He presented the image of a professor rather than that of an astute businessman, yet it was he who ushered in the era of book clubs. After patiently hearing out my story, Scherman made a call to his advertising manager. At the door appeared a fair-haired young man of moderate height who was introduced to me as Harry Abrams. I showed him my picture series "Reading and Books in Graphics and Painting." He seemed interested and mentioned the idea of using them as bookmarks for members of the Book-of-the-Month Club. The fee we agreed upon was one hundred dollars, a true bonanza and food money for me in those early days. Whether or not the prints were ever used, I don't know. Maybe young Abrams bought them simply out of the goodness of his heart—and in sympathy with a coreligionist. As for me, I was delighted to have made the contact, and I kept in touch with my early benefactor, who went on to found the mighty Harry N. Abrams art publishing house.

Clinching my first big order.

ENCOURAGED BY THE Book-of-the-Month Club sale, I set out to look for other prospects. As I wasn't exactly the pushy type, this "doorknob turning" was difficult for me. Often I fell victim—as we all do at times—to that "what's-the-good-of-it?" feeling. But my ego and my financial squeeze spurred me on. Perhaps behind the next door I would find a prospect, I told myself.

This is just what happened when, after a few weeks of persistent pavement pounding, I found myself before the glass door leading into the establishment of a Madison Avenue art and print dealer, Erich Herrmann. This guy will probably give me the cold shoulder, I thought apprehensively. But a surprise awaited me. A highly cultured gentleman and a personal friend of many artists (among them George Grosz), Herrmann welcomed me warmly. Eager to help, he gave me the telephone number of a publisher, a Mr. Austin (his first name escapes me—his firm has long since vanished), who had visited him that very morning in search of illustrations for a forthcoming world history. It was just the lead I needed.

I called Austin and he invited me to his office in the Empire State Building, in those days a rather forbidding place for a newcomer from Europe. But at last I had made it to the fortieth floor of a skyscraper. More importantly, Austin became my first big customer. He was what is called in the trade a subscription publisher, selling books "by the yard"—not to read but to fill up shelves, in no way an illegitimate business. His latest project was a world history in ten volumes. To make the series more attractive, he had planned a pictorial insert for each volume. It was a project made to order for me.

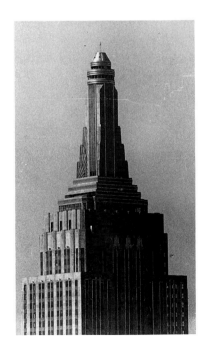

After outlining his plan, Austin asked me how much I wanted for such an assignment. After a painful hesitation, I said—no doubt with a tremor in my voice—"Seven hundred and fifty dollars." He seemed stunned by the price, and I thought I had blown my chance by being too greedy. But then he replied, "Let's make it an even thousand, it sounds better," and it was my turn to be stunned. It was the first (and last) time in my long career that anyone offered me a larger fee than I had asked for.

The assignment was completed in good time and to Austin's satisfaction. The twelve-inch-wide series of books in green embossed leather looked rather handsome, but I often wondered how many buyers would bother to read them or look at the pictures I had assembled.

The encounter with this bookman, my generous benefactor, ended on a rather ugly note. In the course of a luncheon in the club at the top of the Empire State Building, I asked Austin where he spent his week-ends. He said he had a lovely place in Maryland, adding: "And the best part of it is"—and these were his exact words—"no Jew ever settles there." I was deeply perturbed by this remark. Hadn't I come to this country to escape such malignities? I had naively thought that such bigotry didn't exist in the land that had given me asylum. I know now that strong undercurrents of discrimination are ever-present, even in America. One has only to think of the pronounced anti-Semitism of the much-venerated mythologist Joseph Campbell. Nevertheless, I can report that overtly anti-Semitic remarks have rarely been uttered in my presence. In these many years since my last meeting with Austin, I have never again had to endure an open slight against my people—an immense blessing when I think of the prejudicial ranting to which I was exposed before I left my homeland.

Surviving on "then and now" picture features.

London suitor rises in "elevator carriage" to pick up his lady, whose enormous hat prevents her from passing through the ground-floor doorway.

WITH THE AUSTIN ASSIGNMENT successfully completed, I thought I had made it. My optimism, buoyed by my new bank account, even prompted me to hire an assistant, a young writer with the appropriate name of Arnold Bennett. Bennett had a flair for combining some of the material in my files to create "picture features." These we tried to peddle to magazines. The *American Weekly*—a Hearst Sunday supplement—was one of our hot prospects. Its picture editor, a retired rabbi named Dr. Samuel Levy, particularly liked features that showed outlandish inventions. When we inquired what he needed, he growled, "Get me believe-it-or-not stuff."

We also began assembling "timely features." Whenever an important news event broke, we tried to provide some historical background by way of our old prints. The Dionne quintuplets of Canada were then much in the news. But multiple births were hardly something new. We could point to precedents via pictorial "news releases," which Sunday supplements at times picked up.

A more ominous event prompted one of our most successful features of that time. In September 1938, the prime minister of Great Britain, Neville Chamberlain, carrying a rolled-up umbrella, scurried off to Munich to mollify Adolf Hitler by trading Czechoslovakia for "peace in our time." In the Western democracies, Chamberlain's appendage quickly became the symbol of craven appeasement, which our picture feature on the umbrella satirized with wry humor.

About this time, a young New York University student, Ernest Kroll, came to me offering to do publicity for the Archive; I think he

Left: A midwife hands to a mother the only surviving infant of quadruplets she has given birth to. The hovering saint takes charge of the souls of the three stillborn infants. Right: The famous Dionne quintuplets of Canada shown with Dr. Allan Roy Dafoe, who cared for them as they grew. The birth of the "quints" (May 28, 1934) prompted numerous requests for pictorial antecedents of this happy event.

"Toenail-cutting machine"—a sample from my "believe-it-or-not" file.

proposed a salary of twenty-five dollars a week. I hired him on the spot. Ernest developed some good ideas. He contacted the *New York World Telegram*—then the leading afternoon paper—and was able to sell them the Bettmann story with the title "His Hobby Grew into a Business." He also managed to interest the forbidding *New Yorker* to take notice of my still-struggling enterprise. Ernest, a fine published poet, became an expert in Japanese and worked for years for the U.S. government in Washington. I am still in correspondence with him.

Boosted by Ernest's publicity efforts, I thought I was also ready to take on sales help on a commission basis. A young woman by the name of Lillian Ross, who was to become a prominent writer at the *New Yorker,* offered to make the rounds if she was paid on the spot for any pictures she sold. When I years later reminded her of our early association, Miss Ross recalled the time she had made a slam-bang sale of five pictures to the *American Weekly* and came back to gather praise and her commission. "When I gave you the good news your face turned white," she recalled. "There seemed to be no funds at hand to reward me." Indeed, I had to wake up and realize that my thousand-dollar bank account was not a permanent fixture. Even in miraculous America, bountiful orders didn't grow on trees.

It soon became obvious that a service providing a historical context for news events did not have a very bright future. In the early days of

Left: Neville Chamberlain carrying his famous umbrella to the Munich Conference in 1937, during which he appeased Adolf Hitler in hope of achieving "peace in our time." This event created a demand for our somewhat facetious feature on the history of the umbrella. Center: Woman escapes her pursuer by floating downward, suspended by an opened umbrella. Right: A poor Parisian poet and attic-dweller fights a leaking roof in an 1848 Daumier cartoon.

the Bettmann Archive, we limped along on these "then and now" features, but today they would have no place in news as we conceive it. A drastic change has occurred in newspaper editing. The immense range of global news to be covered today leaves little room for background features explaining how things came to be. And yet historical perspective is today perhaps one of our most critical shortages.

Finding a competitive edge in a crowded field.

IN MY EARLY professional forays I had become, without quite realizing it, a contender in the photo agency field. I soon had to face the fact that I was by no means the only purveyor of historical pictures. Competition is at times painful but not altogether unhealthy. It's the American way to get to the top. The Brown brothers had been prime photo reporters and recorders of the Gilded Age. Wise enough to keep and organize their impeccable eight-by-ten glass plates, they had long since established "Brown Brothers" as an important photographic credit line.

And there were others. Max Peter Haas had started his European Picture Service. Arthur Brackman and his wife, a most astute photo manager (I was to think of her as the Queen Elizabeth of the picture business), had put Freelance Photographers on the map. Excelling in up-to-date Ektachromes, they also covered the historical scene by purchasing European collections and other picture morgues. Perhaps closest to my own line was the agency that a Philadelphia newspaper-man, Jay Culver, had set up in the 1920s. Culver Service specialized in old photos relating to stage and screen. It also offered an impressive coverage of American history.

With such an alignment of competitors, I wondered at the time whether there was room for another historical picture service. It seemed that American journalism and publishing had limped along quite successfully without this newcomer muscling in. But what else was I to do? I took consolation in the thought that my background as an art historian and librarian might enable me to make a fresh contribution to American picture research. I was, in typical Germanic fashion, an incurable "systems man." By training, I seemed destined to plan the Archive like a library, offering quality pictures assembled according to a logical system. This distinguished my budding enterprise from that of my colleagues—most of them practical yet highly competent journalists.

The careful cross-indexing system that I had developed in Germany was an elaborate, time-consuming procedure requiring patience as well as budgetary support. But it gave me a decided edge over my competitors. In time, the system was simplified somewhat, but the criteria for pictures to be included in the Archive have always been strict ones. I tried to apply to my picture acquisitions the critically appraising eye of an editor. Members of this harassed species have little time to wade through a stack of pictures that are not of the highest order, graphically or in subject matter. Editors needed—and the Archive sought to supply—pictures that told a story, communicated an idea, or reinforced the accompanying prose dramatically, appropriately, and, we hoped, memorably.

At times we lost a sale because we were too critical. I recall a conversation I once had with a colleague, Thomas Healy, who ran a small historical picture agency. In a friendly way he disputed my theory that a good collector must be a ready "thrower-awayer." ("The best is a foe of the good" is the German saying I quoted to him.)

When I next saw him, Healy boasted that he had made it into *Time* with a picture of Napoleon looking like Hitler. "It took me all day to rummage through thousands of prints, but I found it," he said proudly.

"Mr. Healy," I replied, "my compliments on the sale. But permit me to say that you lost money. This isn't quite the way I want to spend my day." Taking into account the fact that impatience is one of the prevailing characteristics in American life—and growing by the minute as our pace accelerates—I found that providing quick retrieval time was of the essence.

By some knack for which I cannot fully take credit, I seem to have succeeded in selecting pictures with a certain offbeat quality, often items that have a humorous effect. Someone once referred to me as the "overlord of pictorial oddities." One of my clients paid me an exceptional compliment when he jokingly observed, "I can recognize a Bettmann Archive print blindfolded."

Arriving at the right place and time: photo reporting in ascendancy.

DESPITE THE COMPETITION I faced, I was still lucky to have landed in this country at a time when pictorialism was very much on the upswing. The United States was, and still is, a country with an appetite for taking in news via the visual medium. Perhaps this has something to do with the country's immensity and fast-paced lifestyle. The impatient temper of its inhabitants means that Americans prefer pictures to the more-difficult-to-imbibe words. No other country has a phenomenon to compare with Currier and Ives, the partnership that produced low-priced prints of more than seven thousand subjects for the American home between 1830 and 1880—the richest and most complete color pictorial record of our national life (even if at times rather sentimentalized).

The enormous success of Currier and Ives was based on the ready acceptance in this country of the "democratic art" of lithography. This printing method was invented in Germany (c. 1796) by Aloys Senefelder, a poor musician who was searching for a way to reproduce his compositions inexpensively. While lithography had a fair run in Germany and France, mostly as an artistic medium, it hit its stride in America when a group of German lithographers settled in St. Louis. By the mid-1800s, it had become a major American reportorial medium. Before photography took over, lithography not only communicated news but also reflected the country's living habits, sentiments, and pride of place.

By the latter part of the nineteenth century, photography had become an important medium of news reporting in the United States. (Even today no other country can match our competence in this field.) In the mid-nineteenth century, it was the new photographic art that recorded the westward movement. The pioneers who made their way to the West after the Civil War were accompanied by a corps of gifted professional photographers. Through pictures, citizens of the East could participate—vicariously, at least—in the settlement of a new territory. Susan Sontag comments on this phenomenon: "Faced with the awesome spread and alienness of the far west, people wielded cameras. It was a way to take possession of places they had discovered."

The inception of pictorialism as we know it today dates from the founding of *Life* magazine in 1936. With a staff of outstanding photographers such as Alfred Eisenstaedt and Margaret Bourke-White, *Life* was an immediate hit, due to its gripping reports of news events and everyday slices of life. *Look* jumped on the bandwagon in 1939. Soon afterwards, World War II became the most photographed war in history. Edward Steichen (who commanded a crew of Navy photographers) and other combat cameramen created heart-stopping images of the conflict. After the war, Steichen would elevate the medium during his curatorship of the Department of Photography at the Museum of Modern Art, which promoted the stars in the fields of fashion, news, and artistic photography.

I had come to the United States at an opportune time—just when the interest in things pictorial was reaching a peak of intensity. Publishers were seeking to support their texts by way of pictures. Magazines opened their pages to picture stories—a journalistic technique freshly enhanced by the arrival of European photographers such as Robert Capa, Alfred Eisenstaedt, and Erich Lessing. Advertisers showed a new interest in graphics and tended toward the pictorial. I had arrived just in time to help them in this direction. Things started to look up in the modest Forty-fourth Street office, but it still was a hand-to-mouth existence. I always had to look for additional assignments. Often they came from unexpected sources.

The first cover of *Life* magazine in 1936 symbolized the arrival of the pictorial age. I was lucky to come to America just when visual documentation was on the rise in the fields of book and magazine publishing.

The allure of pictures is anticipated in *Faust* by Goethe (1852). To capture the hero's soul, the devil tempts Faust with an image of the world's most beautiful woman, Helena. She appears alluringly in a magic mirror—anticipating today's television screen.

Above: A Daumier lithograph shows Parisians of all ages attracted to a display in front of an artist's workshop. Right: A balladeer of the eighteenth century stirs the crowd's emotions by pointing to pictures of heinous crimes. A fiddler's scary scratching provokes hysterical screams from one of the onlookers.

Right: To relieve tedium, Civil War soldiers peer into a "viewing box," which displays a succession of humorous (and perhaps scandalous) illustrations.

Top left: Amateurs were caught up in the wave of pictorialism, causing an increased demand for cameras. George Eastman filled it by introducing the comparatively lightweight Kodak camera, employing photographic film rather than cumbersome glass plates. This made photography a hobby accessible to all.

Top right: Pioneer photographers captured vistas only Native Americans had ever seen before. Easterners eagerly awaited pictures of those wonders from the newly acquired territories out West.

Sidelines: I become curator of a "barbering museum."

Top left: New York barber pole of early 1900s announces enviably low prices and offers showers to the homeless roaming New York streets. Top right: Peter the Great forcing Russians to cut their beards, symbolizing the country's attempt to join the world of western Europe.

IN LATE 1937, I came across a *Reader's Digest* article titled "Why Not Get Interested?" It dealt with a Charles de Zemler, proprietor of an impressive twenty-five-chair barbershop on the ground floor of 30 Rockefeller Center. This aristocrat of barbers had become bored with simply cutting hair and wielding the razor. To add some stimulation to his life, he had begun studying the history of his calling and had assembled a large and unique collection of documents and instruments relating to barbering through the ages. *This is a man I must meet,* I thought, after reading the story.

De Zemler, a fine gentleman of Swedish descent, was delighted to show me around his tonsorial parlor, which looked more like a museum than a barbershop. There were pictures displayed on the walls, and all manner of barbering memorabilia and tools, mugs, and soap covers crammed the show windows. Soon we found a way to collabo-

rate: he assigned me to appraise and catalog his treasures and so to further research on the history of barbering.

Barbering has a fascinating past. It is linked closely to the history of medicine. Medieval doctors didn't deign to dirty their fingers and perform operations. These were left to the lower-class barber-surgeons. Theirs was medicine's "bloody work." Although disdained, some of these lowly practitioners rose to eminence. Among them was Ambroise Paré, a sixteenth-century barber-surgeon and pioneer in the treatment of gunshot wounds. His philosophy is expressed in his memorable motto: "I cut . . . God heals."

Once I had put de Zemler's collection in order, I suggested that he write a book that would feature his treasures and personal memories and would incorporate some of my research findings. His *Once Over Lightly,* anecdotal in style, was the first publishing venture I was involved in in the United States, although I didn't seek or receive credit.

Top: Frontispiece of the ghost-written book *Once Over Lightly: The Story of Man and His Hair.* The book featured Charles de Zemler's collection of barbering memorabilia and my research on the profession. Left: Shaving mug, ca. 1880. Bottom left: Seventeenth-century shaving knife with elaborately designed silver handle. Bottom right: Women operate a tonsorial parlor in downtown New York (1895).

A tentative effort at public speaking.

Forced to lecture, I entertained my young female audience with "funny old prints" from the world of fashion. Thomas Rowlandson's cartoon (ca. 1800), captioned "A little tighter," caused much merriment.

DURING THE ARCHIVE'S early days, curatorship of the de Zemler collection was not the only stopgap assignment I took to help me keep afloat. I also pursued a tip that I had picked up about a potential lectureship at New York's McDowell School of Fashion Design. I gave a sample presentation to the school's owner-director, Lynn McDowell, following which I was hired. Happy as I was to have the job, I was absolutely petrified at the prospect of appearing before a young and critical audience. I was inexperienced in public speaking, not to mention that I still felt awkward in English and was by no means an expert in the field of fashion.

The class I faced was full of giggling girls who, it seemed, expected to be entertained rather than instructed. I had collected as much anecdotal material as I could find on the history of fashion, but I had a hard time putting it across. The girls seemed most amused not by what I said but how I said it. My accent was a source of constant hilarity.

The situation reminded me of a story told about the Hungarian psychoanalyst Sándor Radó. At one time Radó had to give a lecture before his American colleagues. He addressed them in what he thought was his best newly acquired English. After he had finished, the chairman remarked slyly, "A fine lecture, no doubt, Professor. My only regret is that none of us quite understood it, for none of us speaks Hungarian."

I struggled through the McDowell lectures for a year before gracefully bowing out, having at least gained a thorough grounding in fashion history in all its capriciousness. The job also enabled me to acquire a great deal of graphic material that would prove useful in my later dealings with fashion houses and department stores.

To this day I am rather wary of giving lectures, and I fend off invitations to speak whenever possible. Nevertheless, man-to-man or, even better, man-to-woman, I am somewhat more successful. Indeed, there are those individuals—young people especially—who find my accent somewhat charming. Combined with my rather ancient age, as well as the great variety of life's vagaries to which I have been exposed, my way of speaking may inadvertently lend a rather exotic air to my philosophical effusions.

It was perhaps in this connection that the head of the graphics department at Florida Atlantic University, Steve Kika, paid me an odd compliment recently. "Why did you come to see me?" I asked, when he wandered into my office in the library at FAU. "No reason in particular," he replied. "I just like to hear you talk." This endorsement notwithstanding, a platform star I will never be.

**A visitor from the New Yorker
makes an encouraging
prognosis.**

BY THE LATE 1930s, after much bungling and some qualified successes, the Bettmann Archive was on its feet—though wobbling at times. An article in the *New Yorker* by Philip Hamburger, the distinguished "Talk of the Town" correspondent, put it aptly:

> One of the many local enterprises for which we must thank Herr Hitler is the Bettmann Archive. The Archive is a collection of some fifteen thousand photographs of old manuscripts, works of art, mechanical devices, historical characters, household objects, and whatnot, intended to tell graphically the story of man and his work through the ages. It was started ten years ago by Dr. Otto Ludwig Bettmann, then head of the Rare Book Department of the Berlin State Art Library. . . .
>
> Dr. Bettmann can dip into his archive and come up with a pretty complete photographic history of almost anything that might pop into your head—Beautiful Women, Corsets, Headaches, Love, Pain, Plumbing, Rain, Shaving, Sugar, Traffic, Umbrellas, or Vegetables.
>
> Dr. Bettmann knows moments of despondency, his colleagues told us, usually when business has slacked off. Then he sits in his office, muttering, "What can we do? What can we do?" Then, likely as not, somebody will call up for a pictorial history of Happiness, and he's a new man. (*New Yorker,* April 8, 1938, p. 14)

Trademark Registered, The New Yorker
Magazine, Inc.

Sampling from the Bettmann Archive's pictorial file on "Happiness."

IN THE EARLY DAYS of the Archive, our picture sales were made mostly to newspapers, magazines, and publishers. But a friend I had made, Allen Klein, an account representative at a medical advertising agency, tipped me off that book publishing was not where the "real money" was. To improve my income, I would have to break into advertising. Whereas textbook houses and newspapers paid five dollars a picture, promotional fees for an ad illustration could go into the hundreds.

The advertising market opened up for me in a fortuitous manner—one of the first sales I made in this area harked back to my German roots. It was one of those strange twists of fate: Among the few items from my father's bibliophilic treasures I was able to save on leaving Germany were ten volumes of the works of Athanasius Kircher, the pioneering technologist. One of these books was his *Phonurgia* of 1650, an ancient leather-bound tome on the science of sound known to me since early youth. It was replete with illustrations of devices for the transmission of speech. One day in late 1937, I took this book from a shelf in my library and came across an illustration showing what struck me as an early—and most prescient—prototype of a radio station. The thought occurred to me that this odd picture might be suitable for a revealing "then and now" presentation—perhaps in an advertisement by one of the leading networks.

Allen Klein, with whom I discussed this idea, suggested that I send a copy to CBS, then under the leadership of Dr. Frank Stanton, a gentleman of acknowledged taste and learning. I followed this advice, and lo and behold, a few days later I received a call from Victor Ratner, the CBS advertising manager. He told me that Dr. Stanton had passed the print on to him and had suggested that he use it as a basis for a CBS advertisement. Ratner invited me over to CBS headquarters, then on Madison Avenue, to discuss the project. He offered me a generous fee and asked me to assemble more data on Kircher's sound-transmission ideas, as well as whatever else I could find by other writers on the theme of sound and its impact.

I was most pleased about this breakthrough into the world of Madison Avenue advertising, and more so when the CBS ad appeared as a double-page spread in *Fortune* magazine and a number of advertising trade publications. This national exposure—reinforced by the Bettmann credit line—did much to make my work known in the field. It was the first time in my saga as a struggling picture man that I was able to prove that old graphics could be used effectively and tastefully in modern promotion.

The CBS ad that helped put the Bett-mann Archive on the map. It appeared as a double-page spread in *Fortune* (January 1938) and exposed the Bettmann credit line in numerous national magazines.

The Kircher ad won awards for CBS and worked out well for my budding enterprise. It made the advertising fraternity aware of a new source of pictures to use—"antiquity to promote modernity." Years later I wrote to Dr. Stanton, thanking him for his help in launching the Bettmann Archive and complimenting him on his appreciation of old graphic art. He graciously replied that he was pleased to be counted as one of the Archive's godfathers.

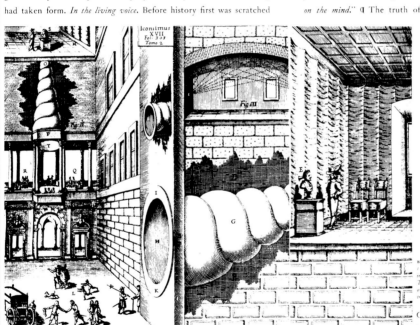

Renaissance courtship.

Give me leave then to refresh my muse a little and my weary
readers with a more pleasing aspersion of love matters.

Robert Burton, Anatomy of Melancholy

3    A MOST

FORTUNATE

ENCOUNTER

MAN DOESN'T LIVE by pictures alone—least of all Bettmann.
When builders of a business (even one as modest as mine) retell their
story, they are apt to recall only incidents pertaining to the commercial aspect of their venture. But there is no doubt that events in the
personal sphere can have a marked influence on the growth of an
enterprise. Experts in autobiographical writing advise that both the
"lived life" and the "felt life" should be recorded. Hence, I ask in-
dulgence for this personal divagation.

The year 1936 turned out to be an annus mirabilis, filled with a
"pleasing aspersion of love matters." I took the initial steps that led
me to a cloudless marriage of more than fifty years. "How did you
meet her?" is the first question people are apt to ask concerning my
marriage—or indeed any marriage. As it happens, my first encounter
with my future wife was rather unconventional.

At that time, Anne Gray (Clemens was her maiden name) worked at
Macy's department store managing the Guilford House, a boutique
specializing in fine antique reproductions. I first saw her when I was
looking for a gift for my friend Paul Jolowicz. Her friendliness,
warmth, and beauty struck me immediately. These qualities were
readily apparent to others as well. Indeed, when my bachelor brother
Ernst first met her, he blurted out, *"Hat sie eine Schwester?"* ("Has
she a sister?")

Anne Gray, the worldly-wise American woman, being wooed by me—admittedly a somewhat stuffy Germanesque scholar in need of a gentle hand to guide his Americanization.

As a rule, German refugees had an unhealthy habit of sticking together. I too had sought the companionship of some of my female compatriots. But I had no doubt that in Anne Gray I had met a genuine, vital American woman. Shy as I was by nature and feeling insecure as a newcomer to this country, I was somewhat puzzled about how to reconnect with her.

I still recall how desolate and abandoned I felt on July 3, 1936, with most of my friends rushing off somewhere to celebrate the Independence Day weekend. With the Guilford House lady at Macy's still much on my mind, I got up my courage and forced myself to call her, though I felt much trepidation. It turned out to be the best decision I have ever made. Anne didn't remember me and had no idea how taken I had been with her on our first encounter. Much later, she laughingly recalled my gurgling voice over the telephone asking abruptly, "Miss Kray [still deficient in my English and feeling very nervous, I mangled her name somewhat], can I see you sometime?" (The subtlety of American dating ploys escaped me as yet.) Anne was a little taken aback—and even more so when I blurted out, "What about tea sometime next week?" Though I must have sounded like an incurable Victorian, to my delight she agreed to meet me the following week to get acquainted.

There was something warm, fresh, and perceptive in this American woman, a quality I had not previously encountered in *mädchen* (girls) of my acquaintance. After our first date, I invited Anne to spend a Sunday with me in Bayside, Long Island, where I summered. She wore a flowery dress I still remember vividly. With her hair parted in front and pinned in a bun at the back, she looked like Wallis Simpson (the American divorcée who became the Duchess of Windsor), though Anne was not as tall. We went to the city park and talked, and I expressed the hope that we might see each other more often. Her reply was unexpected: "You shouldn't get entangled with me. You see, I have three children." Her husband, Zundel Gray, a successful Boston real estate man, had fallen on hard times during the depression and had died of tuberculosis the year before. But the news that Anne was a widow with three children did not have the effect on me she had anticipated. The happiness I felt about our prospective friendship led me to state without hesitation, "Anne is still Anne"—a quote that she always cherished.

It was the beginning of a happy, though at first decidedly underfinanced, courtship. When I picked up Anne in the evening at Macy's to accompany her home, we would treat ourselves to a toasted English muffin at Bickford's Cafeteria. Later on when things had improved, we laughingly recalled these encounters in genteel poverty.

Anne got along well with my friends. I think that they secretly envied me. Surely they realized that American women were a very desirable species, refreshing in their independence and practical outlook. But the idea that I would marry Anne seemed never to have entered their minds. When I announced the news to Paul Jolowicz (the man who had been responsible for our meeting in the Guilford House), he shook his head in disbelief, mumbling, "I have seen strange things happen in my life."

Anne and I were married on March 4, 1938. I became stepfather to Anne's three children—"a ready-made family," as I boasted to my friends. Beverly, my stepdaughter, was fifteen, and my stepson Mel was seventeen; as time went on both became essential helpers in the building of the Bettmann Archive. My eldest stepson, Wendell, was twenty and already on his own as a student at Harvard. He is now a successful philatelist.

Despite the warnings of my friends about getting involved with a woman with three children, my marriage to Anne was a crucial turning point in my life. For more than fifty years I enjoyed the richness of her companionship. In the Archive's early and at times precarious days, she backed me with unflagging belief in my entrepreneurial vision. Indeed, her support and advice emboldened me in my resolve to succeed.

Anne shortly after our marriage—at the entrance of our modest two-family home in Jackson Heights, Long Island, New York.

A MOST FORTUNATE ENCOUNTER

AFTER OUR MARRIAGE, Anne continued to work. We commuted together—Anne to Macy's and I to my office on West Forty-fourth Street—from our small but pleasant two-family home in Jackson Heights, Long Island. We traveled into the city via the Queens subway, a hellish commute in the summer. It would be two years before we could afford our first car, a four-hundred-dollar used Buick.

My parents, still living in Nazi Germany, caused us increasing concern. By 1939, their stay in Leipzig had become extremely precarious, with the anti-Jewish atmosphere growing more threatening with each passing day. Hitler had begun his foreign conquest earlier that year with the annihilation of Czechoslovakia—after the betrayal of that tiny democracy by its erstwhile allies Britain and France. And the führer continued to declare his intention to make the world *judenrein*.

Once again my American cousin Alfred Bettman of Cincinnati stepped in to help. Aware of my parents' plight, he sent them affidavits of financial responsibility, the first step toward emigration. With thousands of German Jews in the same desperate straits, the prospect of escape seemed very slim—especially since the U.S. State Department was tepid, to put it mildly, regarding the prospect of a massive Jewish influx from Europe.

Mercifully, my marital status opened up an unexpected avenue of rescue: my marriage to Anne, an American citizen, permitted me to obtain my own U.S. citizenship in three years rather than five. Having applied when I first arrived, I received my citizenship papers in 1938. This in turn enabled me to apply for the immigration of my parents on a preferred quota. They were finally able to escape Germany via Italy in November 1939, practically on the last ship out. All they had with them were two suitcases and the clothes on their backs.

My parents during their last trip to their native Thuringian Forest, where our family had settled in the 1820s after the Napoleonic era had freed the Jews from confined ghetto living.

One can imagine the human drama that unfolded when I brought my parents to the safe haven of our home in Jackson Heights. I can still picture Anne, home from her job to welcome the new arrivals, falling into an embrace with my mother as the door opened. It was love at first sight, and the two women became tenderly devoted to each other.

As for me, a slight apprehension was mingled with my joy and gratitude. I had informed my parents while they were still in Germany about my happy marriage, but I had remained silent about the three children who comprised the rest of the family. This may well seem fainthearted, but I had feared that my parents would make the totally fallacious assumption that I had fallen victim to some kind of man-eating American flapper. Trying to break the news to my mother gently, I cleared my throat and began to mutter, "Mother, I still have a secret to tell you—three secrets, actually." "What is it?" she asked, a bit concerned. "Have you got three dogs you haven't told me about?" My mother was a woman of vast and loving understanding, and it should not have come as a surprise to me when she not only readily accepted but affectionately welcomed our family setup. By that time only Beverly, the youngest of Anne's children, lived with us, and she became fast friends with my mother.

After a two-week stay with us, my parents moved to the considerably more commodious house of my brother Ernst in White Plains, New York. My mother continued to enjoy the coffee klatches with old Leipzig friends that Anne hosted at our house from time to time. While my mother generally managed her new life well until she passed away in 1951, my father was never quite able to adjust to American ways. He missed his little professional empire—his *Klinik*. His advancing case of "X-ray cancer" claimed his life in 1942, only three years after his escape from Germany. This was tragic, but how grateful I am that my parents were among the fortunates who escaped the horrible cataclysm of the Holocaust.

Bettmann Archive shows signs of life: attracting clients in a domestic setting.

OUR HOME IN Jackson Heights was a modest one, but making ends meet was sometimes a struggle. Once when I had failed to pay the sixty-five-dollar rent by the thirteenth of the month, the usually well-disposed landlord, Sam Frank, showed up red in the face, demanding his money on the spot. Meekly, I somehow scratched the sum together. After this shortfall, Anne, with her astute practical sense, suggested a possible solution. "Let's try to combine home and office," she

The combination living room and bedroom of our Fifty-seventh Street apartment also served as a reception area, where clients (scant in number) were welcomed to the Archive.

THE RISE OF MODERN EUROPE

A GENERATION OF MATERIALISM

1871–1900

CARLTON J. H. HAYES

The first textbook assignment I handled at Fifty-seventh Street. Professor Carlton Hayes of Columbia University (later to become ambassador to Spain) made himself at home in our "domestic office" when consulting me on the illustrations for his book, *A Generation of Materialism*.

suggested. "That way we can get something fairly classy." She always was "in quest of the best."

The "best" within our budget was far from grandiose, but the location of the place we found was just right: a railroad apartment at 215 East Fifty-seventh Street. The premises looked rather dark and dusky; only two large windows, one in front and one in the back, provided sunlight and ventilation (no air-conditioning in those days).

We liked the elegantly decayed decor of this apartment: two fireplaces, high ceilings with old-fashioned moldings, and paneled windows. It seemed just the right setting for the antique furnishings, which Anne and I both preferred, and for the antique pictures, with which I was trying to make a living.

Having left Germany relatively early, before the high tide of Nazism, I had managed to bring over some of my family's furniture, including both my grandmother's Biedermeier desk and—miraculously—my grand piano. My holdings and the antique furniture that Anne had assembled fused well into a home-cum-office establishment. Still, for a time it remained a tight squeeze financially. My stepdaughter Beverly recalls the constant cry whenever money was running short: "We've got to sell the piano!" Fortunately, we never reached those dire straits.

The Archive was growing, but slowly. Yet in spite of our scant success, news of our existence was getting around. Our location proved perfect for a nascent picture agency—right in the middle of New York's art establishment, crowded with antique shops and art dealers. This was worth personal sacrifices. By day, the front living room doubled as office and music room, dominated by my grand piano. By night, it became a bedroom, when we unfolded the sofa bed. Despite the room's multiple functions, Anne's tasteful decorating seemed to enchant visitors.

An A&P market was located directly across the street, next to the famed antique galleries of French and Company. Every day starting at five o'clock in the morning, trucks would unload their cargo with an unearthly racket. This noisy chore was usually finished by eight, but busy Fifty-seventh Street was never without tooting horns.

A trickle of visitors turned up, welcomed with a friendly purr by our doorkeeper-cat, Rusty. Most callers expected a businesslike setting but quickly adjusted to the homey atmosphere. My afternoon and evening clients could always smell what was cooking for dinner in the nearby kitchen. Who knows? It may have helped sell pictures. I remember Carlton Hayes, a prominent Columbia University historian

Anne's daughter, Beverly, who was trained as an artist, joined our home-office operation in 1940. Our cat, Rusty, purringly welcomed clients to the Archive.

and later U.S. ambassador to Spain, visiting me shortly after we had moved in. He needed pictures for his *A Generation of Materialism* in the Harper series titled *The Rise of Modern Europe*. Professor Hayes settled down comfortably in a New England high-backed chair, while I brought him some sherry and then ran back and forth to a rear cubbyhole to fetch pictures for his inspection. The transaction was completed in good time, and the professor was greatly pleased. However, before his arrival, Anne had begun taking a shower, and the bedroom/living room was inaccessible to her as long as he stayed. Clad only in a towel and anxious to get dressed, she waited in the adjacent bathroom for more than an hour.

Although we led a busy, cheerful life in our new apartment/office, our logistical problems were such that we needed a change. One day in 1943, a solution came our way unexpectedly. Our superintendent, the stern Herr Otto Metzger (a compatriot), informed us that the owner had decided to modernize the building and convert from coal to a more effective oil heater. This meant that the dusty coal cellar was for rent. The space consisted of two rooms, close to one thousand

Seated at my grandmother's Biedermeier desk, I inspect new acquisitions under an electrified oil lamp from Anne's American antique collection—a symbol of our happy German-American symbiosis.

square feet, and the rent was twenty-five dollars a month. We pondered this offer at length. Our pictures were bringing in only three dollars to five dollars apiece then (today they are billed at one hundred dollars or more), so Anne and I decided to split expenses. She would open an antique shop in the back room of the coal cellar, and the Bettmann Archive would be established in the front.

Doing business in a converted coal cellar.

AN ANTIQUE SHOP and a historical picture archive seemed well mated, and our new space had some practical advantages. A staircase and a small anteroom led into the dual establishment, and there were two half-sunken windows facing Fifty-seventh Street. On the negative side, as I soon found out, the sewer in front of the windows collected the dust from the street several inches thick. It was a real mess that I had to clean out every so often or face a lake of water from the clogged drains.

To counter the coal cellar's dour ambience (if a coal cellar can be said to have such), we painted the rooms white and enlivened them with plants and displays of pictorial curiosities. A growing number of customers, as well as some purely curious passersby, dropped in and seemed charmed. "This is just what an archive should look like," one visitor remarked. The place became a kind of modest landmark on Fifty-seventh Street. The location didn't hurt either—we were right next to the arty Sutton movie house.

Left: The Fifty-seventh Street entrance to the former coal cellar that was to house the Bettmann Archive. Right: Subterranean picture librarian at work. Fifty-seventh Street dust collected outside my window, clogging the drains. To avoid seeing the Archive flooded during rainstorms, I had to climb out often to clean up the mess.

While Anne's experimental business of selling fine antique accessories had nothing to do with pictures, her shop was congenial and modestly successful. People dropped in from the street to browse—some even to buy. On weekends we would make forays to antique

Anne in an upbeat mood after the sale of her antique accessories to Bergdorf Goodman.

shops in New England or Pennsylvania. I browsed for old photos, while Anne looked for tasteful accessories she thought would sell.

Her enterprise got an unexpected break when Bergdorf Goodman's antique buyer got wind of her tiny establishment (there is no antique department in the present Bergdorf, but of late they have an expanding men's department—such is the march of practicality). It was during World War II, a time when European antiques were in rather short supply. The Bergdorf buyer looked around Anne's shop and seemed impressed by the small but select assemblage of goods. "Would you mind if I buy everything?" she inquired of the startled proprietor. Mind? We were delighted. This grand-slam sale enabled Anne to establish herself in her own shop on the corner of Fifty-seventh Street and Second Avenue.

The Archive, always pinched for space, moved into the vacuum. The former antique shop became a picture-file room that filled up speedily. I had made a beginning with selling pictures. Now I had the elbow-room to acquire more pictures to sell.

Tapping new picture sources: old magazines, slides, and trade cards.

TO GROW AND THRIVE, any business must have an adequate inventory. The added space I had acquired in the coal cellar provided the room to expand. I was faced with a dearth of pictorial documents, particularly in the nineteenth-century American vein. But this deficiency was soon to be overcome, for I discovered the enormous richness of America's graphic tradition and tapped that resource eagerly.

Between 1850 and the advent of halftone reproduction in the early 1890s, America produced a number of magazines profusely illustrated by wood engravings. While somewhat rough in nature and lacking a photograph's lifelike veracity, these illustrations added up to a unique record of American life—political and social. Copyright restrictions on all these magazines had lapsed, so the illustrations could be used freely. *Harper's Weekly,* highly pictorial in its makeup, enjoyed nationwide success; it was the *Life* magazine of its time. The rival *Leslie's Illustrated Weekly,* founded in 1855, was even livelier. No wonder, for it was edited for a time by the spirited Miriam Florence Leslie, the author of *Are Men Gay Deceivers?* (1893).

When I started the Archive, such magazines were still available for as little as five dollars for a full year's run. Today single-page illustrations may be found in antique shops with a price tag of twenty-five dollars and up. While *Harper's* and *Leslie's* stuck to facts, a more daredevil note was provided by back issues of the *Police Gazette,* from

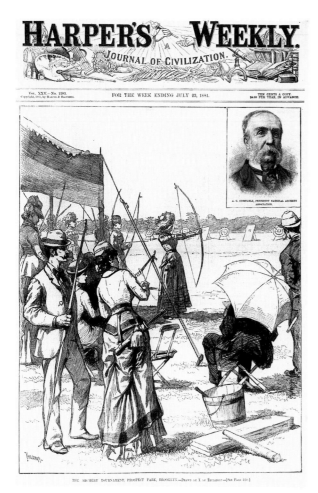

ALMOST TRAPPED.

AN EPISCOPAL MINISTER IN NEW YORK JUST MISSES BECOMING THE VICTIM OF A HORRIBLE AND SCANDALOUS
BLACKMAILING RACKET.

Left: Typical cover of *Harper's Weekly,* one of America's highly successful family magazines, and an inexhaustible source for illustrations of nineteenth-century life. Right: The *Police Gazette* covered the more lurid side of New York. The issue shown here told the story of an Episcopalian minister who was almost lured into the den of a New York streetwalker (1886).

which I also eagerly excerpted picture material. Virtually unobtainable today, this magazine, printed on roseate paper, was the favorite reading material of barbershop customers. Its animated pictures dwelled on highly unsavory or titillating (for those naive times) situations, with an editorial pitch similar to that of today's *National Enquirer.*

I cut these picture accumulations apart. Family members helped me with the chore of mounting. I must admit I wasn't totally sold on the idea of covering the American scene, a field in which I had strong competitors. But Anne wisely insisted that I go for full coverage in my picture collection—and I am glad she did. There is always room for one more competitor, if he or she can find a way to "do it a little better" (the old Emersonian mousetrap idea).

Perhaps coming fresh to this field enabled me to unlock picture sources yet untapped. The most surprising discoveries I made were in the field of old lantern slides, which at the time were still available for a pittance. The lighting of a "lanterna magica" was a high point in the entertainment schedule of the Victorian family. Indeed, the projections on a white tablecloth were humble precursors of our life-size

Above: "Body and soul are mine," said he. "I'll have them both for liquor." The devil bewitching people with drink, in a slide from a mid-nineteenth-century temperance lecture. Right: A father enthralls his children and their friends with a "magic lantern" show. The projector flashes an early commercial on the wall. Below left: Pro-temperance lantern slide shows a dissolute crowd in a New York bar—including a drunken mother with a baby. Below right: The assassination of President Lincoln. From a slide series on Lincoln's life by Boggs Beale, a famous Philadelphia lantern slide artist.

television screens. During the Gilded Age, lantern-slide production attracted considerable artistic talent, yielding pictorial Americana accessible nowhere else: color illustrations of literary works (*Ivanhoe, Ten Nights in a Bar-Room,* and *Uncle Tom's Cabin*), humor, fairy tales, and moral preaching. Thus these old lantern slides add to our understanding of "the good old days," both their charms and their curses (poverty, slavery, alcoholism, child abuse).

Trade cards, an early form of advertising by nineteenth-century merchants, were another picture source as yet untapped. The four-by-six-inch cards often bore bizarre and outlandish pictures. They became the object of rabid collecting among Victorian children, who glued the finds into weighty scrapbooks. In the 1940s I could still acquire one of these collections at a pittance. The hefty tomes went

Cigar-box graphics offered a rich lode of pictorial oddities. Such artwork often seemed to anticipate the extravagances of pop art.

right into our bathtub to be soaked until the individual cards floated to the surface. Of course, I did not keep every card but fished for those with some "subject significance" or outlandish design.

The trade-card field's most popular items were those showing the greats of baseball, issued by tobacco manufacturers at the turn of the century. In today's auctions they have become the object of passionate bidding. A multicolored baseball card depicting Honus Wagner, the great shortstop of the Pittsburgh Pirates, was sold in early 1990 at Sotheby's in New York for the somewhat astounding sum of $451,000. Who knows if a similar treasure may not still slumber in the bottomless files of the Bettmann Archive?

When I opened the *New York Times* not long ago, I noticed in the music section a half-page reproduction of a Viennese ballroom scene, credited to the Bettmann Archive. I remember that this came from a trade card I had acquired for five cents in an antique shop. Of course, I should be humble about such incidents—conscious as I am of the thousands of pictures from magazines, slides, and trade cards that I assembled in the Archive's early days but, alas, never sold.

Buying from collectors: the illusion of hidden treasures.

IN 1980, when I sold the Archive to the Kraus–Thomson Organization, the Canadian publishing conglomerate, there were some three million items in the inventory. After Kraus–Thomson took over the collection, it absorbed the enormous morgues of United Press International and Reuters and grew to some twelve million images. At times, I can't help exclaiming, like Samuel F. B. Morse, "What hath God wrought?" Perhaps this is the place to answer the question I have been asked time and again during my long incumbency at the Bettmann

"When three beats to a bar became magic." Trade cards of the 1890s often showed pithy real-life pictures, like this Viennese ballroom scene that was recently used as a half-page illustration in the entertainment section of the *New York Times*.

Archive: "How the devil did you manage to assemble such a huge number of pictures?"

It all began with the first picture I snapped when I was rare book curator in Berlin. Since then, I have pursued "picture bagging" with mad persistence, not unlike Vladimir Nabokov netting butterflies. Picture hunting became a way of life, requiring enormous effort and dedication on my part. I have been a lifelong subscriber to the theory of Arthur Schlesinger, Jr. When this teacher, historian, writer, and former presidential adviser was once asked how it was possible to wear all these different hats, he replied with a smile: "Gentlemen, does not the week have seven days? Does not the day have twenty-four hours?" I will admit I have pursued pictures with a round-the-clock passion—or one can call it madness if one is less charitably inclined. With a husband always involved in his business, such workaholism may cause problems. I will admit that Anne, herself a professional woman always involved in her own work, still might have missed at times a full measure of marital companionship. However, only on rare occasions did she observe, with an ironic smile and in good humor, "My husband is always at the desk."

I cannot claim to be personally responsible for all of the Archive's growth. Sometimes pictures walked, figuratively speaking, into my office. Almost daily we were visited by collectors and "lucky heirs" who, bringing offerings in bags or portfolios, enabled us to extend our files into areas still inadequately covered. I remember one man coming in with a thick scrapbook containing nothing but tobacco graphics.

A MOST FORTUNATE ENCOUNTER

At work taking pictures with the Leica camera stand. With this simple device I took thousands of pictures in libraries and museums all over the world to increase the scope of the Bettmann Archive.

The contents were garish and naive, but seductive in their blazing color: a kind of early pop art. Cigar-box covers, cigar bands, and tobacco ads—all ephemeral subjects and hence doubly hard to come by—were pasted together in his weighty volume. It was almost too much of a good thing—no doubt lovingly accumulated by an inveterate smoker as a tribute to a vice that would be his undoing. We photographed the essential items and resold the volume at auction. Antiquarian booksellers often brought in similar accumulations of clippings, old family albums, and scrapbooks with trade cards or illustrated ads.

I sometimes found myself in the uncomfortable position of having to disillusion amateur collectors about the value of their offerings, which they regarded as rare treasures. This puncturing of dreams happened most often when heirs offered "invaluable" old glass plates. Typically they were shots grandpa had taken, perhaps during the Spanish-American War, and as a rule worthless for our purposes.

With due respect to grandpa, his shots generally lacked the sharply focused, close-up action today's editors demand even in old-time photographs. The fact that a picture is old did not necessarily make it valuable or worthy of inclusion in the Archive. Snapshots lacking focus and good composition simply didn't make the cut.

I had to be equally harsh with callers who offered "valuable old books." The date on the title page is not as a rule a true indication of a book's worth. Worthless books were produced by the millions in the past just as now. They were trash when they appeared, and trash they have remained. Even books with a classic—even a holy—content often prove to be valueless.

I always got a little impatient when a solemn voice announced over the phone: "I have for sale a Bible that has been in our family for over a hundred years and is decorated with valuable engravings." Such family Bibles have been produced by the thousands, and booksellers won't even offer five cents for them. People also are inclined to think that books illustrated with woodcuts and engravings must have a special value, but one should keep in mind that these are mostly mass-produced items. Very early, limited-edition imprints are, of course, measured on an entirely different scale. A volume illustrated by one of art's greats, a Degas or a Picasso, will bring big money in auction, and of course so do very early imprints or rare first editions.

Although I turned away many offerings, I profited from the steady influx of picture material that came to me unsolicited. One great find out of hundreds examined made the process worthwhile.

Have camera, will travel: trudging through libraries the world over.

IF I ACQUIRED MUCH picture material from previous owners and amateur collectors, my own research trips also contributed greatly to the Archive's growing inventory. My Leica was always at the ready. In the Archive's early days, when resources were still on the skimpy side, I often had to hustle to fill incoming requests—especially those from the news magazines, whose picture editors were an impatient and demanding bunch. But the appearance of our credit line in such national media as *Time, Newsweek,* and *Life* was worth a special effort.

I remember *Time* once asking for a picture showing Sykes, the rascal in Dickens's *Oliver Twist,* which I didn't have in my collection. Undaunted, I packed my portable reproduction setup and rushed out to catch the number 20 bus on Fifty-seventh Street to the New York Public Library on Fifth Avenue. In the Reading Room I ordered illustrated editions of the novel and photographed what seemed to fill the

The calamitous death of the villain Bill Sykes in *Oliver Twist*—a Dickens illustration I had to hustle to deliver in time to *Time* magazine.

bill. Then I rushed back to my office, quickly dried and copied the film, and had the approval pictures ready for *Time*'s messenger at three o'clock. I forget now whether I got into that edition, but I knew this was a case of "better to try and fail than to fail to try." My "express service" was observed with some amazement by my stepdaughter, Beverly, who was then working with me. The next time a similar situation arose and our own resources let us down, she suggested with a smile, "Why don't you run down to our little annex on Fifth Avenue?"

As time went on, I made many research trips to line up picture material in out-of-town libraries and historical associations. None of my picture-search expeditions were packed with more excitement than my forays into the Library of Congress in Washington. I found the resources of its Prints and Photographs Division to be staggering— some 12.4 million items were stored there. Moreover, I was fortunate enough to be received as a colleague by the department's curators, who gave me free access to the stacks. Thus, I was able to roam its picture-crammed expanses at my leisure, coming home with a rich harvest of Americana.

Of course, the bounty of pictures I photographed myself or ordered had to go through the usual process of subject analysis, grouping, and cataloging to make the newfound Americana available pronto to our impatient clients. They clearly saw the advantage of coming to us and getting instant service (for which they gladly paid) instead of engaging in a search and correspondence with our national library—venerable, inexhaustible in its resources, but of necessity slow to respond to outside requests. (Plans are now underway to change this situation and turn our great national treasure into the nation's foremost public data base, accessible via computers and other information-processing technology.)

During my various excursions to Europe—which were planned as pleasure trips—I generally fell victim to my picture mania. Though picture sources in France, England, and Italy are truly unlimited, access to them is in no way as liberal as in the United States. Yet the picture harvest I brought home always proved an invaluable addition to my stock. From the Bibliothèque Nationale in Paris, for example, I brought home an almost complete collection of portraits of France's great personalities in the arts and literature by simply selecting and having copies made from hundreds of negatives taken by the great French photographer-balloonist Nadar (1820–1910).

A pictorial bonanza: views of the Lower East Side.

LIKE THE BIBLIOPHILE who never ceases to dream of a once-in-a-lifetime find—the proverbial multimillion-dollar Gutenberg Bible at a bargain price—the picture collector always hopes for a lucky break. Sometimes it happens.

Who would have thought that a New York homeopathic physician on West Ninety-sixth Street would on his death leave behind a remarkable visual treasure trove? In June 1958, I received a call from a man who said he was an heir of the late Dr. J. William Bartlett, whose estate contained a large collection of slides and negatives. The doctor's house and the accumulations of a lifetime had to be sold. The heirs were anxious to get rid of the boxes and boxes of "junky glass plates" collecting dust in the attic.

Like an old hunting dog sniffing rabbit tracks, I made haste to answer the call. With one look at the accumulations in the Bartlett attic, I knew I had made a lucky strike. The slides and negatives revealed scenic views of New York's Lower East Side of impeccable pictorial excellence. Packed with human interest, the images offered a unique panorama of late nineteenth-century street life and the immi-

Top: Immigrant life in New York's Mulberry Bend: a young mother makes a purchase from pushcart peddler. Middle: In the Italian section of the Lower East Side, a shoeshine boy is confronted by one of "New York's finest." Free shine coming up? Bottom: A gang of boys scheming at mischief in Mulberry Bend. Some of their descendants may have ended up as doctors and Wall Street brokers. (Photos by J. William Bartlett).

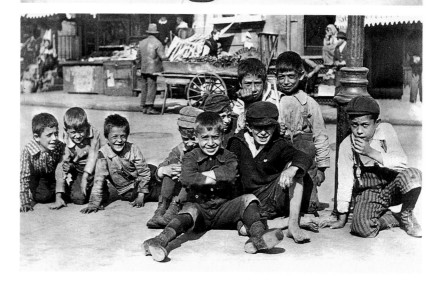

grant settlement at Mulberry Bend. I could readily see that these pictures were superior in subject matter and quality to the famous Riis photographs, which were of a similar vintage. But the Riis photographs are almost unrelievedly grim—the photojournalism of a reformer who wanted the world to confront the poverty in which "the other half" lived. Bartlett, on the other hand, often caught the district's inhabitants in more playful moments, at times of relaxation or high spirits—thus providing a more complete record of life as it was lived, to the fullest, on the sidewalks of New York.

Dr. Bartlett had been fascinated with life in this most colorful part of town. I learned from his heir that many a Sunday he packed his camera to catch Mulberry Bend people at work and play. Though an amateur, the good doctor had a remarkable feel for what Cartier-Bresson called "the decisive moment." What made this find doubly valuable was the fact that the shots had never before been publicly shown. Dr. Bartlett simply took pride in exhibiting his Sunday harvests via projected slides to his friends and family. When I asked the impatient heir how much he wanted for the lot, he said, "Give me fifty dollars and drag it away."

Exploring newfound treasures is one of the thrills of this business, further sweetened if you can envision a ready market. I lost no time putting together a feature called "Dr. Bartlett's Mulberry Bend," and sold it to the *Saturday Evening Post*, which published it in August 1958. If the businessman in me was pleased with the very impressive profit earned in the transaction, the photo historian in me was even more pleased to bring Dr. Bartlett's fine work to the attention of the American public.

Artists predict the future with startling prescience.

AS I BUILT UP the Archive, a specialized field came into my purview and demanded attention. I had noticed that we received frequent requests for predictions of "things to come"—science fiction was obviously America's cup of tea. Indeed, a market had existed for pictorial futurism almost since the inception of the new republic. I concluded that a special file on graphic science fiction would find ready takers and set about to create such a section as a subhead in our "Engineering" file.

One would think that science fiction literature would offer ideal illustrative material in this vein, but a stab in this direction proved futile. In the novel *Looking Backward* (1887), Edward Bellamy—a strong critic of the Gilded Age who yearned for the creation of a better

Trumping Trump: in 1892 the humorous magazine *Judge* spoofed the growing trend of building sky-scrapers in New York City, picturing a huge edifice that offered its residents every conceivable facility—meat markets, museums, a fire department, and a racetrack—all serviced by an ascending spiral railroad.

A medieval vision of the artificial creation of human life: Homunculus ("little man") takes shape in a retort, as the alchemist looks on.

Self-portrait of Albert Robida, graphic futurist, from *Magazine of Art* (1899).

society in the future—had predicted among other miracles the invention of the radio and the packaging of precooked meals. Of the former invention he commented: "If we could devise a gadget providing everybody with music at home, suited to every mood, we should have attained the limit of human felicity." And indeed this felicity we have attained—as well as many other unforeseen benefits. Unfortunately, Bellamy's works had no illustrations. *Oh well,* I thought, *Jules Verne's books no doubt contained some spicy graphic material.* But thumbing through his works in New York's French Library—a part of "L'Alliance Française"—I found little that was pictorially exciting. Then, like the biblical David looking for a lost sheep and finding a kingdom, I found science fiction pictures of an amazing and spirited kind in the work of the French artist Albert Robida (1848–1929). This lucky find amplified the Archive's resources and resulted in many sales.

Robida was the quintessential science fiction artist. In thousands of drawings made between 1870 and 1900 for books and magazines, he prophesied the technological and biological advances of the late twentieth century. He envisioned television, helicopters, tape recorders, submarines, and even test tube babies. His drawings were equally prescient when it came to predicting social changes, from women's liberation to the rise of weekend leisure trips and televised education. Robida also foresaw the grim side of the future century, with dark visions of gas warfare, overpopulation, and the replacement of the book by "discothèques."

There is an interesting sidelight to the Robida saga that Edward Tenner, executive director of Princeton University Press, explored in his article "The World's Greatest Futurist," published in *Harvard Magazine* (January–February, 1990). Tenner asserts that Robida's vast artistic output reflected not a hopeful anticipation of the future, but rather a wish to debunk the future before it arrived. Actually he wanted to show how confused and fearfully complicated the future would turn out to be, and he hit the nail on the head. Indeed, to reinforce the fact that Robida was actually an antifuturist, Robida's son reported that when his father died in 1929, he had never made a telephone call, ridden in an automobile, or come close to an airplane.

Modern times predicted by nineteenth-century French futurist Albert Robida.

An 1882 cartoon by Robida predicted the advertising media of the future: a spray gun peppers the city with circulars, while the balloon promotes mustard and shoes.

Thieves arrive via balloon to pilfer an attic apartment.

A young woman comfortably ensconced at home takes a university course by "telephonoscope"—an 1882 lithograph that accurately forecast the offerings of public television.

Below: An aerial taxi delivers a woman to her balcony on her return from a successful shopping trip to town. Top right: Predicting television: a Parisian lounging at home watches an opera-ballet performance. Bottom right: A televised report—"via telephonoscope"—on war in Africa is watched by a family in their living room.

Top: I consult with Bradbury Thompson, a leading graphic designer, about a picture problem. In front of me is the Archive's picture guide, which is divided into forty-seven categories (from advertising to zoology) with more than two thousand subdivisions. Bottom: *Westvaco Inspirations*, a style-setting publication on graphic design, was art-directed for many years by Bradbury Thompson. The issue shown here marked the beginning of our collaboration.

4 "YOU EITHER GROW OR YOU GO"

A poster given to us as a moving gift by one of our clients, New York art director Ron Barrett.

"KEEP IN MIND, my dear man, in America you either grow or you go." Such was the advice my friend and self-appointed guardian, Mike Lebaur, gave me one day in early 1960 in our Fifty-seventh Street coal cellar, where we had happily done business for close to twenty years. It was a crucial bit of insight for me, even though it came from a man who knew nothing of the picture business. Lebaur was an American lawyer who was smart enough to know that nothing stands still in our country. I took his hint to heart.

It was time to abandon our "old curiosity shop" and move the Archive fully into the twentieth century. Our next locale was to be on the eleventh floor of a modern skyscraper, the Tishman Building at 136 East Fifty-seventh Street. The new location was just a block away from the old coal cellar but a world removed in atmosphere: Alexander's and Bloomingdale's animated the neighborhood, and fine antique shops abounded. The Archive had moved smack into the middle of New York's bustling commercial and artistic center.

Looking back, I am amazed that we accomplished this major move without more severe financial pangs. As a rule, any growing enterprise needs seed money for expansion, yet in my entire career I have never had to resort to a bank loan or taking in a partner. The Archive just grew, leavened by some mysterious yeast.

To underscore the impression that the Archive was up-to-date and "with it," Anne decorated our half-floor (later to be expanded to a full one) in a decidedly modern style. *Interior Design* magazine featured it in one of its issues. "It looks more like IBM than an archive," one visitor observed. When Friedolf Johnson of *American Artist* magazine paid us a visit, he wrote in his report that he had expected an archive to be a musty, dusty place. "The only dust I could find was my own," he joked, "on the top of my shoes."

Our new setting was subtly contrapuntal. Old graphics served up via wall displays in a thoroughly modern setting proved attractive not only to the community of art directors but to picture seekers in many other fields as well. But it was not only a matter of improved ambience; doubling our space enabled us to work more efficiently and expand our resources and photographic facilities.

Welcoming visitors to the Archive's new home was a continuing enrichment for me. Some clients were prominent personalities; others, simply respectable workers in the field. Some were to become friends for life. (How fortunate I was that I had slipped into this sort of business, not condemned to being a purveyor of pork bellies or gear-cutting machinery.)

One day a slim man in his early thirties came in to rummage through our files of movie stills. He signed in as Johnny Carson and explained that he was trying to develop visual gags for his TV show. He was deadly serious in the pursuit of his quest, and it was somewhat of a disappointment that he did not regale our office staff with funny quips.

In 1964, the artist Larry Rivers explored our resources in Russian history for a projected (and successfully completed) mural on Russia. We charged a research fee of thirty-five dollars—an incredible bargain—but all I remember is that we had a hard time collecting the money.

Andy Warhol, the maven of pop art, never visited us personally. However, he once sent an assistant to get a picture, not for reproduction purposes, but purely for "inspiration." For such a use we made a ridiculously modest charge: five dollars. What he made of it probably sold for thousands. It wasn't long before a check arrived from "The Factory" signed by Andy Warhol himself. I wish I hadn't cashed it. Alas, who can see around corners?

Dr. Alfred Kinsey visited us to acquire picture material for the Institute for Sex Research that he had
founded at Indiana University (1941).

Left: Medieval chastity belt used to
enforce a woman's faithfulness during a knight's absence. Center: The
Greek physician Galen (A.D. 129–ca.
199), surrounded by a group of students, instructs a young couple on
the techniques of intercourse. Right:
Greek vase (4th century B.C.) showing couple during erotic play.

OUR COLLECTIVE PULSES began to pound when we received a
letter from the Institute for Sex Research at the University of Indiana,
announcing that the famed sexologist Dr. Alfred Kinsey wanted to
visit the Archive to add a historical section to his own picture archive
(which, according to its present director, Margaret Harrer, has now
grown to forty thousand items).

The first Kinsey report of 1948, *Sexual Behavior of the Human
Male,* had offered statistics that at the time proved sensational. Even
more shocking was Kinsey's second volume (1953) on the human
female. The latter revealed that twenty-six percent of all married
American women had engaged in premarital sex—a statistic that
surely needs overhauling today. The impact of the so-called Sex Doctor (a zoologist by training) has been described by an early associate,
Dr. Wardell Kaster Pomeroy: "Kinsey sought to help the individual to
cast off the primary thing his parents had taught him—that it was
immoral to enjoy intercourse: homosexual, heterosexual, premarital
or extramarital."

We were well prepared to accommodate Dr. Kinsey. In the early
1930s, back at the Kunst Bibliothek in Berlin, I had been the curator
of an outstanding collection of erotica assembled by the German sexologist Edward Fuchs (1870–1919). One of his best-known works
was a heavily illustrated three-volume tome titled *Broad's Domina-
tion of the World (Die Weiber Herrschaft).* Fuchs can be called the first
sexological pictorialist (or pictorial sexologist). In an attempt to keep
them out of the hands of youngsters, some of the volumes were re-
leased by the publisher "for adults only." I had photographed some of
this material in Germany and it was filed in our "Section 20," which
contained erotica of all types, ranging from the more conventional to
the outrageous. Dr. Kinsey selected quite a few items from among the

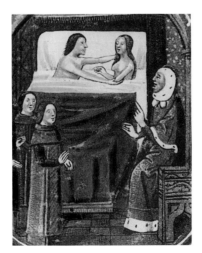

Venus and Vulcan, by a Renaissance painter of the Fontainebleau School. I sold a contemporary copy of this painting to Dr. Kinsey, who thought it most appropriate for the entrance of his Institute for Sex Research.

formerly "forbidden fruits." I must admit that the "daring" pictures I brought from Germany would likely impress us today as naive. For better or worse, we have learned a lot.

Since my apartment was close by, we invited Dr. Kinsey over one afternoon to meet some of our friends (who were tactful enough not to probe him with questions that had to do with his field of unsurpassed expertise). At one point Dr. Kinsey, a modest and basically retiring man, excused himself from the assembled crowd and wandered into my library. There he noticed a large copy of a painting that I had brought back with me from a trip to Italy. Ascribed to the late-sixteenth-century Fontainebleau school, it depicted a highly erotic version of the Venus and Vulcan theme. Dr. Kinsey was fascinated by it and asked me if I would sell it to him—it would be ideal for the entrance to his institute, he said. As my interest at the time tended more toward things American, I was in a selling mood; needless to say, measured by today's prices for original art, Dr. Kinsey got a bargain. I asked him for a thousand dollars, and he readily accepted.

Our erotica file has undergone a considerable increase in use, especially since the appearance of popular magazines that have explored the field with candor. One of the pioneering ventures was Hugo Gernsbach's *Sexology,* to which we often contributed. Later on, even *Hustler* occasionally requested our help. Of course, sexual mores have changed a great deal since I began collecting. Nevertheless, the Archive's erotica collection—strong in depicting sex life in more restrictive times—remains much in demand. Who knows, we may be ready for a return to romantic love, the real thing—another theme thoroughly covered by the Archive. As Somerset Maugham put it, "Love makes the wheel of the world go 'round—and money greases its axle."

Edward Steichen selects Bach manuscripts to decorate his music room.

WE FELT PARTICULARLY HONORED when Edward Steichen, the doyen of American photography, paid us a visit. Steichen was responsible for creating the unparalleled Department of Photography at the Museum of Modern Art and initiated the all-time best-selling picture book based on the exhibit "The Family of Man." What in the world could the Bettmann Archive have to offer him? Steichen in need of pictures seemed like Morgan in need of cash.

Steichen was tall and slim, imperial like an Old Testament bearded prophet, yet cordial in his manner. It turned out that he had come to us searching for some graphics he could use as a wallpaper in the music room at his estate in Ridgefield, Connecticut.

Edward Steichen, the eminent photographer, came to us in search of pictures for the walls of his music room. He decided on a composite of Bach manuscript reproductions.

Manuscript of Bach's *Violin Sonata in G*—a graphic recording of the workings of a great mind.

We thought at first of portraits of composers but quickly rejected the idea as too corny. When I happened to show Steichen my collection of Bach manuscript photo reproductions, his eyes brightened. As is well known, Bach was a gifted calligrapher with a powerful style of script—the undulating strokes of his pen reflecting the up-and-down oscillations of his mind and at times resembling abstract art. Thus, it has been said with justification that Bach wrote *Augen Musik* (music for the eye).

Attracted to the expressive power of the manuscripts, Steichen hit on the idea of using some of them as an abstract wallpaper pattern for his music room. I hasten to repeat that all the Archive had to offer were photo reproductions of Bach manuscripts. If I had been in possession of even one page in the master's original hand, I wouldn't have had to run the Bettmann Archive—I could have retired. (Original Bach manuscripts would bring millions today at auction—if they were at all obtainable.) Yet this man wrote music by the ton—more than one hundred volumes in the *Neue Bach Ausgabe*. His usual fee for a Sunday cantata was twenty-five *thaler* (about twenty dollars in the good old days).

Speaking of skyrocketing prices, Steichen's photographs have not done badly either. In a February 1991 article in *Connoisseur* magazine, a collector proudly reported that he had acquired one single early Steichen photograph at the bargain price of $195,000.

A debate on words and pictures with Barbara Tuchman.

I OFTEN ENCOUNTERED people of note during my forays into local libraries. Among these emporiums, one of the finest in atmosphere and resources is the New York Society Library, a luxurious converted townhouse on Seventy-sixth Street filled from top to bottom with literary treasures. This aristocratic haven, which houses many

Barbara Tuchman, Pulitzer Prize–winning historian, discussed with me the relative merits of words and pictures as historical evidence.

works on New York history, became my almost daily beat during the writing of my book *The Good Old Days—They Were Terrible*. One of the acquaintances I made there was Barbara Tuchman, the Pulitzer Prize-winning author and historian—a woman of keen intellect and quick wit. She frequently did her research at a desk reserved for her in the second story Founder's Room, an antique-filled wood-paneled chamber. Not surprisingly, we once got into a discussion of the old controversy of words versus pictures as sources of historical information.

Tuchman embarked instantly on a defense of the literary medium, pointing to the usually static quality of pictures as opposed to the endless pliability and fine shadings inherent in descriptive words (which, it is common knowledge, she handled with consummate mastery). I must have surprised her when I, stereotyped as the "picture man," declared, "Mrs. Tuchman, I couldn't agree with you more." Indeed, it always comes as a surprise to people when I confess that despite my lifelong involvement with pictures, I consider words infinitely superior as a means of communication. In his book *Exiled in Paradise: German Refugees and Intellectuals in America*, Anthony Heilbut comments on this idiosyncrasy of mine: "Bettmann . . . even within the hermetic domain of his archival kingdom . . . has maintained a familiar emigré distrust of images."

True, pictures reflect action superbly, but rarely do they reflect thought. It has been said that photos are something one instantly admires and instantly forgets. A photo of Lincoln giving the Gettysburg address conveys a setting. To comprehend the miraculous working of Lincoln's mind and his linguistic genius, one must read the

Gettysburg address. Of course, the best of all possible worlds is to have both images and pictures working together—not only the text of Lincoln's immortal speeches and writings but also the images of the man himself and of the great civil conflict with which he struggled.

Master merchandiser Stanley Marcus—a connoisseur of art and fine books.

THE VARIETY OF PEOPLE knocking at our door always amazed me. Our clients included members of New York's publishing and advertising crowd, out-of-town textile manufacturers looking for new patterns, designers of children's games, and Harvard scientists.

Stanley Marcus, renowned as a creative merchandiser, came to me in search of illustrations for his autobiographical book, *Quest for the Best*. I found myself in the paradoxical position of trying to "unsell" this peer of salesmanship. After we discussed the book's theme and his picture needs, I asked him, "Mr. Marcus, you have so many current accomplishments to relate and illustrate, why burden your saga with historical images?" Apparently I made my point, for in the end he illustrated his book more symbolically and evocatively with engravings depicting tradesmen wearing the tools of their profession. This gave the book graphic unity and subtle class—the quintessential

Below: Stanley Marcus's home in Dallas attests to his wide-ranging interests as a reader and book collector. Right: An itinerant printer of the seventeenth century. Copper engraving.

Marcus quality—and *Quest for the Best* became a best-seller (as had his previous memoir, *Minding the Store*).

When Stanley Marcus wasn't "minding the store," he indulged his passion for books. Since I was of the same persuasion, we established an immediate rapport. After his retirement, Marcus established the Some Such Press, which published fine miniature books. His own collection of more than five thousand rarities of this genre gathered during his worldwide travels was displayed in an acclaimed 1978 exhibit at the Library of Congress.

Though I never sold Marcus a single picture, we have kept in touch over the years. When I recently visited Dallas, he arranged a party for me, during which I had the opportunity to meet his family and some prominent local writers. The Marcus home has the ambience of a fine art museum—its ample wall space is almost entirely taken up with artwork and shelves of valuable books. Stanley Marcus is exemplary in his ability to combine merchandising genius with the pursuit of the spiritual and the finer things in life.

Archive grows by purchase of entire collections—but this method has pitfalls.

IN THE ARCHIVE'S early days, I attended book fairs and auctions in search of fresh material. I also continued my visits to libraries with my camera at the ready, and purchases from individual collectors contributed much to our stock.

Our spacious new Fifty-seventh Street quarters permitted a more efficient way of expanding our files. Now we were able to consider the acquisition of entire photo morgues or of a photographer's back files. When a photographer decided to quit or a newspaper ceased publication, the inventory that became available invariably tempted us to make a pitch. Buying whole collections seemed so much simpler than building up our stock piece by piece. Alas, here too wrinkles could develop. No deal is all good. Each one is apt to have unfavorable aspects.

New vistas seemed to open when my charming French colleague, Philippe Gendreau, dropped by in early 1967 and causally asked if I wanted to buy his picture agency. My dream had always been to extend the coverage of the Archive into the present, and Gendreau's agency seemed to show some promise in realizing that objective. It was a modern picture agency, strong on what is called stock shots—everyday depictions of cars, family situations, offices, etc. Gendreau had been in business for forty years, accumulating a valuable back file. Most of the photos—all taken on eight-by-ten glass plates—were of

A tourist of the thirties departs from a hotel in France. A typical vintage picture from the Philippe Gendreau Collection we had acquired.

the finest quality. Gendreau had covered the French realm particularly well, from medieval cathedrals to modern-day life in the countryside. We quickly settled the deal for what even in retrospect seems a substantial amount of money.

Looking back, I sense it wasn't my wisest decision. I didn't realize that if I wanted the Bettmann Archive to become a "modern" picture agency, I would have to have a constant influx of current material, and the Gendreau Collection was static. (The goal of making the Archive a truly modern photo agency was only realized in 1984, when, as noted earlier, the Kraus–Thomson Organization linked up with the United Press International and Reuters agencies.) At the time of its acquisition, the Gendreau material was neither old enough to fall within my own specialized field of collecting nor current enough to qualify as truly contemporary. So I must chalk up the Gendreau purchase as a qualified boo-boo. One can't win them all, but such failures must be balanced against unexpected lucky strikes. In his book *Up the Organization,* Robert Townsend—for a time president of the Avis car rental chain—admits that he considered himself lucky if out of ten executive decisions he had to make, three proved workable.

Even if one errs in estimating the value of old photos at a given time, solace may come with the passing of years. David Greenstein, the Archive's current director, tells me that with the revival of interest in the Truman years, "Gendreau has come to life again." Such unforeseen revivals are no rarity.

During a recent visit to the Bettmann Archive, I spent some time roaming through the files of oversized pictures that I had acquired for a song. Among these pictures I discovered an eleven-by-fourteen photo entitled "A Night View of the Piazza San Marco." This photo was recently reproduced in *Connoisseur,* with the comment that it had sold at auction for fifteen hundred dollars. Think what the original plate would be worth if anyone could locate it today! Once I bought a collection of fine photographs from a New Jersey woman for thirty-five dollars. The six unwieldy volumes, which I lugged home on the subway, depicted Egyptian life in the 1860s as shot by the pioneering French photographer Bonfils. These scenes, eagerly sought by modern collectors, would easily be worth thousands of dollars today. Such acquisitions were just lucky accidents—I can't take credit for prescience. Patience, the passing of time, and changing markets have brought about the appreciation of value. It is gratifying to know, however, that the present owners of the Archive have bought not just a business but a collection that will continue to rise in value.

Underwood and Underwood: boy wonders.

Bert Underwood, who with his brother Elmer founded the photo agency of Underwood and Underwood. During World War I, Bert headed the photo branch of the U.S. Signal Corps—a position similar to that held by Edward Steichen in the U.S. Navy during World War II.

LOOKING AROUND FOR sizable acquisitions, I was quite excited when I heard in March 1972 that the morgue of the old Underwood and Underwood photographic house was to come on the market. This was an incredibly rich accumulation of negatives and prints from the late nineteenth century to World War I. The collection seemed tailor-made for me, and my mouth was watering. I was crushed when I learned my offer had been topped by another bidder, George Rinhart, a collector of vintage photographs. But all was not lost. We were able to persuade Rinhart to turn the Underwood files over to the Bettmann Archive and grant us the right to sell their contents on a commission basis. This arrangement has worked out well over the years.

This collection has a fascinating history. The firm of Underwood and Underwood was founded in Kansas in the 1880s by Bert Underwood, then eighteen years old, and Elmer Underwood, age twenty. These young fraternal entrepreneurs had anticipated the growing popularity of stereoscope views—twin images that gave the illusion of depth when viewed through the stereoscope device invented by Oliver Wendell Holmes in 1861. This viewing device became part of every household, much like the television set is today. So great was the demand for these needle-sharp pictures that by 1890 Underwood and Underwood produced twenty-five thousand of them every day. Views ranged from vistas of the West (for which Americans always had a

"YOU EITHER GROW OR YOU GO"

Top left: The Underwood brothers created thousands of stereoscopic views of foreign countries. In nineteenth-century America—when only the wealthy could go abroad—middle-class families traveled vicariously by viewing these 3-D photographs of foreign lands. Top right: A stereoscope. Invented by Oliver Wendell Holmes, this device enabled the viewer to perceive duplicate photographs in three-dimensional depth. Left: A weight watcher of the early 1900's. Women of the period were so heavily dressed that it was said their clothes sometimes weighed more than their bodies. Above: This genteelly titillating bathroom scene is typical of the stereoscopic genre pictures made popular by the Underwood brothers.

Above: Four University of California runners challenging the iron horse. From the extensive Underwood and Underwood sports file. Right: The Underwood and Underwood files on William Howard Taft—America's heaviest president—helped us to create a popular feature on weight watching and dieting. After an illness, Taft told Secretary of State Elihu Root that he felt well again and had ridden twenty-five miles. Root laconically replied, "How is the horse?"

craving) to humorous shots and Gay Nineties scenes. The double negatives yielded perfect paper prints, though the scenes of daily life smacked a bit of the sterility of wax cabinet figures. At the turn of the century, with the stereoscope market in decline (by 1910 the rage had totally collapsed), the Underwoods went into the news photo business and scored again. Soon the credit line "Underwood & Underwood" dominated the newspaper field. Having this collection within our bailiwick proved to be an essential addition to our coverage.

Ready access to Underwood photographs dating from the turn of the century enabled me to indulge an old predilection of mine. I had always enjoyed offering new perspectives on current social trends by assembling subject features based on photographs and artwork of bygone eras. One example of this was the feature I put together on the American obsession with weight watching that has become so prevalent in recent decades. The picture series I developed on this timely topic found a ready market among the manufacturers of diet aids.

I "accept" Hollywood: a joint venture with movie publicist John Springer.

ACQUISITION AND COMMISSION deals continued to be made over the years. Some of them were negotiated by Melvin Gray, my stepson and inventive associate, who had joined the Bettmann Archive in 1965. In this area and others, Mel made essential contributions to the growth of the Archive. He was trained as an engineer and had acute business instincts, so his qualifications complemented my own scholarly leanings. We made a good team. Indeed, it was Mel who helped me to acquire the rights to the Underwood and Underwood morgue and to integrate those holdings into our own files.

In the late 1960s, Mel had met John Springer and learned of his extraordinary collection of Hollywood material. Personally, I wasn't a great fancier of Hollywood. I thought that collecting still pictures—turned out by the thousands by the great movie production companies (MGM, Warner Brothers, Columbia Pictures, etc.)—was a little beneath our dignity. However, with the rise of a worldwide film culture, I eventually changed my mind. I came to realize that film was indeed an important twentieth-century art form that mirrored the passing scene, often with pungent humor. Today I am a rabid film fancier, though I have trouble finding enough good movies to indulge my fancy.

Mel arranged for me to meet John Springer, and without further ado a deal was struck and a lasting friendship formed. A leading film publicist and author, John had begun collecting movie stills when he was only ten years old. A friend of his family—the manager of the

The enigmatic Garbo. The Springer Collection is rich in still photography from the golden age of Hollywood, when the studios produced thousands of glamorous publicity shots of movie stars. To this day, they are unsurpassed in their genre.

Left: An early Hollywood director, working with a camera vastly different from today's sophisticated filmmaking equipment.
Right: This famous Harold Lloyd movie still of the "clock hanger" was used by *Time* magazine (October 15, 1990) to dramatize the idea of "high anxiety."

Park Theatre in Rochester, New York—gave him promotional photos of his heroes Tom Mix and Rin Tin Tin and of the object of his preadolescent adoration, Nancy Carroll. As early as high school, John began writing about movies—mostly, he now admits, to get on the mailing lists of Hollywood studios. The promotional photos continued to pour in through college and during his career as publicist to the stars—among them Burton and Taylor, the Fondas, and Paul Newman and Joanne Woodward. By the late 1950s, his collection was so large it cluttered his New York apartment as well as his offices in London, Rome, Paris, and Los Angeles.

All along, John had been lending out photos for free. When *Life* once sent him a check for one thousand dollars for a single story, it dawned on him that his collection could be earning its keep. Mel convinced him that the Bettmann Archive would be the logical agency to catalog and administer the vast collection. He had the pictures, we had the marketing setup. Moreover, the level of mutual trust was such that when I asked John if we should draw up a contract, he replied, "Don't send a lawyer, just send over a truck."

The collaboration has been very successful. "I don't have to worry about my collection," John noted recently. "The Archive pays me a commission on pictures sold, and four times a year the check comes—and has for twenty years."

After we were given custody of the Springer Collection, we developed a specific file of gag shots, which early Hollywood deliberately or by accident produced in profusion. These hilarious photos were often used as attention-getters in ads, mailing pieces, and even on the covers of national magazines. They became particularly popular when shown to enliven monotonous stretches at sales meetings—at times poking some good-natured fun at management or the company's workers.

Digging for pictures that just don't exist.

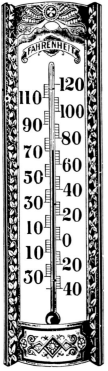

Above: The name Fahrenheit appears on millions of thermometers, but I could not track down a picture of the man who in his own time was considered merely a humble instrument maker—hardly a personage worthy of being immortalized in print or paint. Right: Steve Leveen, president of the *Tools for Serious Readers* company in Delray, Florida, was impressed when we answered his request for a medieval reading stand by sending him a photograph of a painting by the fifteenth-century German painter Michael Pacher. It shows the devil himself, with obvious disdain, holding up the Bible for Saint Wolfgang, Bishop of Regensburg.

EVEN WITH ITS RESOURCES constantly growing, the Bettmann Archive wasn't able to fill every request. It is difficult to come up with a picture that doesn't exist.

Sometimes our customers asked for the impossible. For example, no one took photographs of Andrew Jackson at the Battle of New Orleans (though we remember his timeless command: "Soldiers, elevate them guns a little lower"). Just the same, we had photo requests for this 1815 battle—which some customers presumed had been fought in the photographic age.

One would think it should be a cinch to provide a picture of the physicist Daniel Gabriel Fahrenheit (1686–1736), the man who devised the system by which we in America measure degrees of heat and whose name is found on millions of thermometers and invoked by legions of worried mothers. But although Fahrenheit became a dominant name in thermal physics, in fifty years of searching I have never found a picture of the man himself. In fact, I made a standing offer of a reward to anyone who could produce any kind of likeness of Fahrenheit. So far, there have been no takers.

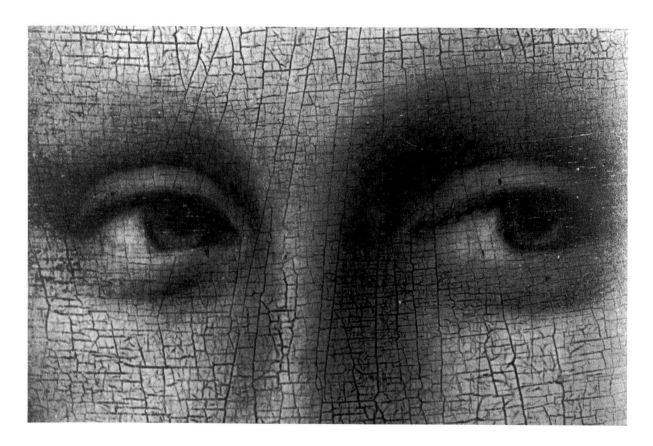

The *Mona Lisa*, one of the world's most famous pictures, is both instantly recognizable and rather hackneyed as an illustration. We provided offbeat caption material to revive interest in this classic picture.

Other requests diligently researched but unfilled were for pictures of the Earl of Sandwich eating a ham-and-cheese on rye and of Spinoza grinding lenses. A jokester, wanting to make some good-natured fun of us, put in a request for Alexander the Great being fitted for a new pair of sandals. Another kiddingly ordered "the *Mona Lisa*—in profile—I don't want that hackneyed old frontal view."

We often tried to compensate for the commonplace aspect of well-known, oft-used, or stodgy pictures by supplying frisky captions to freshen them up. The caption we supplied with the *Mona Lisa,* for example, noted: "When this painting was stolen from the Louvre in 1911, Bernard Berenson, the great Renaissance art expert, observed: 'An incubus—I was glad to get rid of it'; Fernan Léger let it be known that he considered the *Mona Lisa* 'as interesting as a can of sardines'; whereas Marcel Duchamp remarked, 'She has a hot ass.'" (The source of Duchamp's information is unknown.)

Outlandish requests speedily filled, thanks to the visual picture index.

THE MORE THE Archive grew, the larger the assignments we were able to handle. Orders of fifty pictures or more for a single textbook were no rarity, but greater things were to come. In the summer of 1963, my office made an urgent call to our home in Pound Ridge,

New York, with news of an order of incredible proportions. "There is a man here who says he wants to buy five thousand pictures," Betty Paulis, my secretary of many years, told me excitedly. I thought surely it was a hoax played by a friend. "As tactfully as you can," I instructed her, "thank the man and tell him to leave."

It proved to be no hoax, however, but a bona fide order for a new twenty-five volume encyclopedia planned by an Argentine publisher, Editorial Abril of Buenos Aires. We received long lists calling for portraits, nature shots, pictures of inventions—everything under the sun. The job involved months of arduous work, but we triumphed. Even though the fee per picture was low, it was a worthwhile order.

A welcome by-product of such odd assignments was the education we gained. Our associates, who welcomed cerebral nourishment as well as monetary income, always tackled these challenges with enthusiasm. A young employee once confessed to me she had imbibed more knowledge of the vital kind in a year at the Archive than she had in four years of college. Speaking for myself, the Archive became "my private Oxford and Cambridge" (to use Melville's phrase for his whaling ship, the *Pequod*). My seat at the picture window of history proved a continuing source of insight and inspiration.

Life was never dull at the Archive. All kinds of editorial assignments came in over the wires—some strange, all challenging, especially picture requests from advertisers. Most of them were marked "urgent" and we responded accordingly, but as a rule we had to wait weeks or months for confirmation and payment.

A cosmetics company once requested a pictorial survey on the subject of itching. Pertinent pictures were to be used to herald a new anti-

Left: Answering a request by a firm that made a product to relieve skin irritation, we submitted this picture of the Napoleonic army (including a female camp follower) engaged in a frenzy of back scratching. Right: A scratching post set up by the Duke of Argyll (1678–1743) on his estate provided another possible illustration to promote our client's anti-itching preparation.

irritant powder. The most amusing item we dug up was a picture of a scratching post and its background story: "To comfort his shepherds who were infested with vermin, the Duke of Argyll equipped his estate with scratching posts. Every time a shepherd scratched himself on one of the poles, he exclaimed with temporary relief, 'God bless the Duke of Argyll.'"

Once the makers of Mott's applesauce sent us a cable: "Send everything you got on apples." A follow-up letter explained that the company was producing a booklet that would stress the folklore and mythology of apples. Thanks to our catalog system, it didn't take us long to respond. Our index and entry "Apples" guided us to a photo of a relief showing the ancient Garden of the Hesperides, where the golden apples were cultivated and jealously guarded until Hercules, in his next-to-last labor, was able to steal them. The apple of discord that led to the Trojan War, amply represented in classical paintings, completed the mythological background. And of course we had a close-up of William Tell ensuring the independence of the Swiss canton Uri by shooting an apple off his son's head. An old print showing children apple-bobbing at Halloween and another of a New York apple seller of the Depression era completed the series with a realistically American touch.

Our most unusual request is one we never actually received, for it was a fictional one. My idea of building up a visual index—so crucial to the success of the Bettmann Archive—had been widely commented

Left: William Blake (1757–1827), detail of *The Temptation of Eve.*
Right: Hercules stealing the golden apples of the Hesperides—the last of his arduous labors.

Above left: Apple-bobbing was a popular game during Thanksgiving parties in nineteenth-century New England. Above right: An unemployed World War I veteran sells apples on the sidewalks of New York during the Great Depression. Right: Swiss hero William Tell artfully shoots an arrow through an apple placed on his son's head (1307)— and gains his canton's freedom from the tyrannical Austrian overlord, Hermann Gessler.

on in library journals and similar publications. It had also become well enough known to be featured in a detective novel, *The Red Fox,* by the Canadian writer Anthony Hyde (Ballantine, 1984). In this exciting yarn, a detective is anxious to identify a person in a photo who is suspected of being the Communist leader Georgi Dimitrov. After consulting various Washington sources unsuccessfully, the hero-detective reports:

Finally widening my search, I got lucky. This was in New York in the Bettmann Archive—the last place I looked—undoubtedly where I should have gone to begin with. . . . The Archive houses one of the largest collections of historical photographs in the world—and they are superbly organized. . . . Instead of making you paw through trays of prints or file folders that end up spilling all over the place, they have a nice neat system of index cards. A small print of the photo is reproduced on one side of the card; there is a brief paragraph of commentary, and then a half dozen index headings. . . . (Ballantine, 1985 ed., p. 148)

So the detective meets up with his man at the most unexpected place—one of our visual index cards. Needless to say, I was rather pleased when, years and years after I had started our system, my good friend Virginia Meyerson, a connoisseur of detective literature, tipped me off to this unexpected tribute to our handiwork.

Humble experiments in sales promotion; we try to practice what we preach.

I MUST CONFESS TO a kind of Jekyll-and-Hyde personality split. Part of me is a laid-back, bookish fellow. Another part of me is congenitally restless and impatient to hear the telephone ring. I have always harbored a gnawing desire to promote the Archive, to compete with the best of them. People have often credited me with a strange flair for publicity. I don't know if I should take this as a compliment or a criticism.

It is a fact that I've garnered praise ranging from articles in various company publications and local newspapers to national magazines: *Time, New York Times Magazine, Newsweek,* and *Connoisseur.* I have also been lured into direct-mail ventures, though now I am inclined to swear when I find my own mailbox stuffed with advertising circulars and junk mail.

Using direct mail to promote a picture service was virtually unknown when I was starting out. My reasoning for considering this

"Man in the doghouse"—a typical Nostalgicard. We used these to promote the use of old photographs in advertising and publicity campaigns.

gambit was that since we were trying to sell our pictures to others for promotional purposes, it was only logical that we should practice what we preach by exploiting our own graphic wares. Our direct-mail efforts—modest at best—have ranged from one-page flyers to elaborate thirty-two-page color brochures detailing the different services offered by the Bettmann Archive. One of the most successful campaigns we staged involved a package of "Nostalgicards," which featured old movie gag shots. We sent the collection around to advertising agencies, inviting copywriters to pen appropriate captions. Prizes were offered for the most humorous entries. *Advertising Age* published some of the funniest examples, giving us further exposure.

Over the years, we discovered that it pays to advertise. The present owner of the Archive, the Kraus Organization, now makes a quarterly mailing of an attractive newsletter laconically called *Bettmann,* with highly satisfactory results, as I understand. Shall I laugh or cry at the abandonment of the word *Archive?* Perhaps I should rejoice at the fact that *Bettmann* has become generic.

The Bettmann Panopticon, staged with the dynamic Peter Max.

Above: Logo of the Bettmann Panopticon. Below left: Max designed a series of psychedelic posters for the Panopticon. They have since become collector's items. Below right: Peter Max and myself in front of a "flip-card" kinescope, part of a collection of early pictorial reproduction devices I had acquired over the years.

IT HAD ALWAYS been my hope to free the Archive from the image of a dusty old place harboring pictorial has-beens. To that end, I have tried to promote new uses for old prints and have encouraged artists to make them part of a modern design. This avant-gardism is an aberration in my nature, which otherwise tends towards the conservative. I guess we are all bundles of idiosyncrasies.

My avant-garde leanings were shared by a young, highly gifted graphic artist I met in the early 1960s—Peter Max. Though he has an international reputation in the art world today, Peter Max back then was just another beginner on Madison Avenue. He discovered the Bettmann Archive not long after his arrival in New York (at age twenty-two), and he frequently drew on our resources for inspiration. "Whenever I would run out of ideas, I'd go over to the Bettmann Archive and ask for the 'Unusual' file," he recently stated when we had a reunion in his palatial studio in the Hotel des Artistes, opposite New York's Lincoln Center. "I'd find bearded ladies, circus performers, giants, midgets, all sorts of oddities, and it would get me going again."

In 1961, Max suggested that we put together a show in which we would display the work of well-known art directors, based on material from the Bettmann Archive. More than fifty of New York's eminent artists were given free run of our files to select an item to serve as a takeoff for an updated design piece—be it a mobile, collage, or three-dimensional construction. I dubbed the exhibit the "Bettmann Panopticon" (*panopticon*: "to see all").

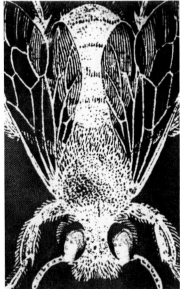

Top left: Photo of young Civil War soldier is given deeper meaning by combining it with a shocking scene from one of the conflict's bloody battles. Panopticon composite by Emil Dispenza. Bottom left: Humorous Panopticon entry by art director Derek Rabinovitch. Right: Spoof on pop art at its height in the early 1960s. An assemblage by art director Jack Wolfgang Beck.

Max promoted the show with gusto, producing a series of posters that are now collector's items. I introduced the show's catalog with a hand-scribbled program note. The exhibit became the basis of a half-hour documentary, *Art for Archive's Sake,* broadcast by the New York public television station. The program, which was rebroadcast several times, featured the artists demonstrating how old graphics can serve as a base for a thoroughly modern design.

Some twenty-eight years after the event, Peter Max acknowledges that the Panopticon exhibit was a major step forward for him. Almost overnight he had become a prominent figure in the New York and international art establishment. Now a world figure, he represents a rare combination of artistic gifts and promotional genius.

5 BETTMANN
THE BOOKMAN

Opposite page: *The Compleat Book-man*, a painting by Giuseppe Arcimboldo (ca. 1530–1593). He is today considered a forerunner of surrealism. Above: "A mighty good sausage stuffer was lost when this man became a poet." Cartoon by F. Opper.

THE "ITCH OF LITERATURE" afflicted me early in life. My native Leipzig was a very literary town, filled with writers, publishers, and international printing concerns; the *Brockhaus Lexikon,* a twenty-volume research tool akin to the *Encyclopaedia Britannica,* was published there. My own writing efforts began in 1928 with my doctoral dissertation; shortly after that, my history of the Rothschild publishing house, *State and Humanity,* appeared. They were not world-shaking ventures, but they were enough to spur me on. When I came to the United States, career interests forced my literary ambition to play second fiddle. Writing a book in addition to directing the Bettmann Archive and enjoying my family life seemed like trying to run a three-ring circus. But the "itch" persisted.

As strong as my compulsion was toward bookmaking, I was not unmindful of the hazards and pangs that accompany authorship—a discomfort that has been likened to childbirth. The poet Stephen Vincent Benét went one step further: when asked how he felt after completing his verse epic *John Brown's Body,* he replied, "It was easy . . . just about as easy as giving birth to a grand piano." Nonetheless, I continued to feel an urge to do a book. I reasoned that some writers have succeeded in leading a double life, engaged in a practical profession and turning books out on the side. Indeed, present conditions make this more a rule than an exception.

Long ago, Anthony Trollope (1815–1882) wrote forty-seven novels and twenty-five other books while leading a busy life as an executive in the British Postal Service. He got up religiously at five o'clock every morning and wrote for three hours. He followed that routine year in and year out, wherever he happened to be (and his job required quite a bit of travel). In his autobiography, still very much worth reading, he summed it up pithily: "A small task—if it be really daily—will beat the labors of a spasmodic Hercules."

I did not arise at five o'clock every morning, but I will admit that my working days were at times crushing. However, bookmaking and archive administration blended well together, complementing each other in a way that gave me rare satisfaction. Indeed, my growing experience in acquiring and selecting graphic material further stimulated my desire to structure my own illustrated works. I felt a sense of excitement at the thought of pulling together picture material based on ideas I had developed myself, rather than fulfilling the needs of others (which was my daily chore).

A nostalgic backward glance at America in the Gay Nineties.

BY THE EARLY 1940s, after about five years in the churning American melting pot, I thought I could handle the pictorial part of a book, but I was still a little uneasy about the text. I concluded it would be best for me to become partners with an established writer.

At the time, Bellamy Partridge seemed a likely candidate. He had written several highly successful books on American life, including *Pardon My Dust,* a humorous account of the early days of motoring, and *Country Lawyer,* which recounted amusing incidents in his father's turn-of-the-century law practice.

Reading Partridge's book *Big Family* suggested to me the idea of doing a nostalgic book on American family life. I would do the research, structure the picture spreads, and provide textual material whose themes reflected a subtly "Bachian" symmetry: Country Life, The Call of the City, Vacation Lure, and Return to the Country. Then, riding on his coattails as it were, I would have Partridge finalize the text and lend his name to the project.

I contacted a book agent, Bertha Klaussner, and outlined the idea to her. She thought it both workable and timely—a welcome antidote to the grim World War II days we were facing. She talked to William Poole, editor of Wittelsey House (then the trade division of McGraw-Hill), and he contacted Partridge. Soon a deal was worked out for a Partridge–Bettmann volume.

Top left: A stockbroker of the "rob-
ber baron" period apprehensively
watches the ticker tape during one of
the frequent panics in American economic history. Top right: Photographer's studio at a nineteenth-century
country fair. The immobilizing
mechanism behind the client helped
him to sit still during the long exposure time. Middle: At a Vermont
cornhusking festival, the finder of a
red ear of corn is rewarded—to the
cheers of onlookers—by a kiss from
the village's hesitant belle. 1882 engraving. Bottom: Miraculous new
steam washing machine is tested by
the housemaid of a nineteenth-
century American family. Woodcut
from *Scientific American*.

In late November 1943, Poole invited me to meet with him in the green McGraw-Hill skyscraper on Forty-second Street. He calmly assured me that all the details had been settled. "Now will we have everything completed by April?" he inquired sternly. (It was November.) "You want this in April?" I shot back incredulously. "That would give me just a year and a half to complete the project." "No, I don't mean April 1945," Poole replied. "I mean this coming April—1944. You have close to four months."

I gulped and agreed to his terms. After scanning thousands of pictures for the final selection and consulting a few times with Partridge, I delivered the manuscript on time for a fall 1944 publication. *As We Were* was met with somewhat muted acclaim. I think we had a front-page review in the old *Herald Tribune*'s book section. Commercially, the book had at best a moderate success; the police did not have to be summoned to control the crowds in front of Brentano's. But for me it was an important first: cracking the field of American authorship.

Every author—particularly a novice—is understandably curious to find out whether he or she has "made it." "Do the bookshops have it in stock?" is the cardinal question. The author dreams of a mind-boggling display in Doubleday's window . . . second and third printings in the works . . . Book-of-the-Month Club selection (or at least alternate) . . . Hollywood nibbles. As a hopeful novice, I couldn't suppress an urge to make the rounds to check which New York bookstores had *As We Were* in stock. I was elated to find some had it available, though not in big piles. At least I was spared the unhappy experience of a fellow German novice author—I think his name was Von Zettlitz—who, like me, had hounded the bookstores, asking the crucial question. At one of the shops, an impertinent clerk answered his anxious query flatly with, "I am sorry. No, Mr. Von Zettlitz, we do not have your book in stock."

"How do you know I am Mr. Von Zettlitz?" replied the wounded author with amazement and a touch of pride. "Now Mr. Von Zettlitz," the clerk countered. "To be perfectly frank, who would ever ask for a book like yours but the author?"

A picture pageant of the National Game—and other American sports.

BEFORE I WAS to scale the more intellectual heights of my most challenging book, *Our Literary Heritage,* I became involved in another book project totally contrapuntal in theme and makeup.

I didn't even have to look for a publisher: A. J. Barnes, head of a venerable publishing house specializing in sporting books, came to me. Perhaps inspired by *As We Were,* Barnes asked me if I wouldn't like to try my hand at a picture book on American sports. He had lined up John Durant, a well known sportswriter, and was ready to let me handle the book's pictorial makeup. It was quite a jump from my newly awakened interest in Henry James (which would be such an important motivation for undertaking *Our Literary Heritage*) to the exploits of Joe Louis. Nevertheless, I told Barnes that I would take the proposal under consideration—even though my ignorance of American sports was profound and my interest in it limited.

In an effort to become truly Americanized, I had gone to a few baseball games with a friend, but he was hard put to explain the

Near right: A rare early baseball card featuring the "Iron Horse," New York Yankee star Lou Gehrig. This four-by-six-inch card was recently acquired by a collector for approximately half a million dollars. Far right: President William Howard Taft attempting a hole in one. Below: America at play, from the title page of the Durant-Bettmann *Pictorial History of American Sports.*

various plays to me. I can't say the game itself excited me very much; there was a lot of waiting for what I was promised would be the ultimate thrill—a home run. I hope no one will doubt my fervent patriotism if I admit that I agreed at the time with H. J. Dubiel that "baseball consists of tapping a ball with a piece of wood, then running like a lunatic."

In spite of my uninformed attitude toward the national game, I was very much aware of the vital role baseball played in American life as a unifying, amalgamating force, binding the country together regionally and socially—a common interest shared by bank president and shoe-shine boy alike. Germany had no similar fervently shared pastime, no natural safety valve for pent-up emotions such as that provided by baseball. I am convinced that the presence of baseball—as well as other popular spectator sports—makes it unlikely for a Hitler-type dictator to gain a foothold in America.

This is a roundabout way of explaining why I accepted Barnes's call to help put together the *Pictorial History of American Sports*. Most of the enduring anecdotes were masterfully retold by my coauthor, John Durant. As for my role, even if I wasn't as deeply beholden to sports as Durant, as a picture maven I knew a good sports shot when I saw it.

The final result of our efforts generated enough interest among the many followers of our national pastime to have a second printing in 1965, more than twenty years after its first appearance. A front-page review in the *Chicago Tribune* (November 30, 1952) called it "a marvelously engaging book."

The Bettmann Archive has always benefited from my book projects. *Pictorial History of American Sports* bolstered our sports files. Research for *Our Literary Heritage* uncovered new pictures of Gertrude Stein, Carl Sandburg, and other literary figures to add to our collection. Bettmann the archivist and Bettmann the bookman worked hand in hand. Also, the publicity created by the appearance of a new book with my name on it helped the Archive to become more generally known.

The healing arts in all ages: a tribute to the great physicians of the past.

I GREW UP WITH the smell of ether pervading my father's clinic and had been fascinated with things medical since my early youth. It seemed a foregone conclusion that I, like my brother Ernst, would enter the medical profession. But fate and the ruinous inflation in the early 1920s decreed otherwise. It was decided in a family council that two doctors in the family were enough. Since I at age eighteen was

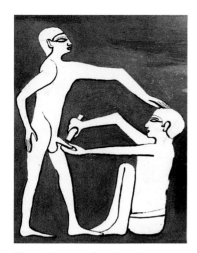

Above: Doctor of ancient Egypt performs circumcision. Right: Early nineteenth-century doctor performs "wayside diagnosis." The setting is a far cry from the gadget-packed consulting room of today's physicians.

already a bookish fellow, it was decreed that I would become an apprentice in a bookshop. For a year I did my daily stint, but I studied assiduously at night, taking classes in history and art at Leipzig University.

Even after becoming established as a "picture man" in America, the medical bug persisted. Finally I was led unconsciously toward a bit of Freudian compensation. I would delve into medicine's past, propelled by the love of a profession that I highly esteemed but was never privileged to practice.

In the early 1950s I sat down and wrote a memo outlining the idea for a book on the history of medicine. As a lark I submitted it to several publishers, not anticipating an immediate response—if any at all. I was also aware that such an all-encompassing book would further tax my already crowded schedule. But at times one has to trick oneself into taking on new obligations that may at first seem beyond one's capacity. As a rule these fears prove unwarranted. The trick in my case was to have a contract with a deadline dangle over my head like the sword of Damocles—leaving me no choice but to get the project finished.

The dramatic appearance of a book publisher, with contract in hand, spurred me into action in the fall of 1954. C C Thomas was as unique and unorthodox as the way he spelled his name. He was the

Above: Dr. Benjamin Rush (1745–1813), prominent Philadelphia physician and signer of the Declaration of Independence, tried to quiet the insane by restraining them in this crude and cruel "immobilizer." Right: Blood transfusion from lamb to man. Engraving from the era of William Harvey (1578–1657), the English physician whose *De Motu Cordis et Sanguinis* (*The Movement of the Heart and Blood*) revealed the workings of the circulatory system. Below: A sixteenth-century woman gives support to her pregnant belly with a barrel hoop.

founder of a well-known publishing firm in Springfield, Illinois, that specialized in medicine, and he had definite, if unconventional, ideas about the publishing business. When I made what seemed to be a reasonable request for an author's advance, he replied sternly, "We have found that if we give advances we never get the manuscript." When I meekly inquired about reprint and paperback rights, his answer was equally unyielding: "We don't grant these rights to another publisher. We will continue to publish a book under our own imprint as long as it sells." I had some apprehensions about this strict regimen, but since C C Thomas seemed eager and willing to make the book a reality, I signed the contract on the spot.

After two years of work, *The Pictorial History of Medicine* was published in 1956, and it was rather warmly received. *Time* reviewed it in a two-page spread, and the *New England Journal of Medicine* and the *Journal of the American Medical Association* applauded it as a "first."

In retrospect, I must say C C Thomas's unconventional publishing methods have served me well. Now, thirty-five years after its first appearance, *A Pictorial History of Medicine* is in its fifth printing and, with little or no promotional push, it still has a trickle of sales. Perhaps the humanistic approach I took has something to do with the enduring appeal of the book. It does not deal so much with the complex technicalities of medicine as with the touching dedication that great doctors have shown their patients. Today, after decades of

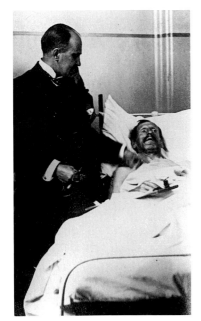

Above: Sir William Osler (1849–1919), "the Great Physician," preached the importance of bedside diagnosis. His *Principles and Practices of Medicine* (1892) was a basic medical textbook at the turn of the century; many of its precepts are valid to this day. Right: An insomniac is fiddled to sleep. From *Medical Housebook of the Cerruti family of Verona*, ca. 1450.

startling technical progress and diagnostic innovations, the medical spotlight seems to turn anew on the patient. As the great doctor Sir William Osler observed, "It is often more important to find out what kind of patient has a disease than what disease a patient has." Perhaps my medical history has remained popular because it reflects this credo.

Our Literary Heritage: the pleasures and profit of working with Van Wyck Brooks.

THE IDEA FOR MY most spiritually rewarding book dawned on me after I had become acquainted with Van Wyck Brooks's monumental five-volume series *Makers and Finders: A History of the Writer in America* (1936–47). This acknowledged classic served as the basis for my collaboration with Brooks on *Our Literary Heritage*, which began right after I had completed *The Pictorial History of Medicine*. The Brooks–Bettmann book was published by E. P. Dutton in 1956.

Transforming Brooks's inspiring epic of "American life seen through the literary window" into a picture book was not just a challenging venture in bookmaking. The project also allowed me to become more thoroughly acquainted with America's literary history, opening my eyes to the enormous artistic and intellectual striving that distinguished the American scene in the nineteenth century.

Europeans as a rule are profoundly ignorant of much of this work. The well-educated German of my generation had only an inkling of Emerson, Melville, and Whitman. (Thoreau is loved the world over,

Above: Van Wyck Brooks. President John F. Kennedy once called him "America's first man of letters." Right: In the climax of Herman Melville's *Moby Dick*, Captain Ahab catches up with the object of his life-long obsession. The white whale symbolized for Melville both the horrific uncaring forces of nature and the "enormity of evil."

Left: Scene from Henry James's tragic short novel *Daisy Miller,* in which a pretty, naive American girl falls victim to the extravagance of the ruling aristocracy in Victorian Europe. Right: Edna St. Vincent Millay in the famed Steichen photograph. Museum of Modern Art.

especially in Russia.) But even as prolific a writer as Henry James was only a shadowy figure in Germany's literary firmament—his brother William, the Harvard psychologist, was actually better known.

It was Van Wyck Brooks, America's "First Man of Letters," who enabled me to supplement my knowledge of German literati with the great figures of American literature. I learned to admire Henry James in particular, not just as a writer but also for the credo expressed in his novels—the way "he took on and took in the world." If I were asked what one book I would choose to have if stranded on a desert island, I believe I would take Leon Edel's panoramic *Life of Henry James,* itself a literary masterwork. (I hope I could also add to my satchel *War and Peace* and *Madame Bovary.*)

In turning Brooks's magnum opus into a picture book, I proposed to follow a procedure similar to that used in developing the Partridge–Bettmann *As We Were* volume. Brooks's publisher, Eliot McCrae of E. P. Dutton, liked the idea and gave his unqualified support.

Brooks had only a faint idea of my background and he indicated that before we began work he would like to become better acquainted with his proposed collaborator. We agreed to meet after Brooks had returned from a European pilgrimage to what he called his "mon-

Robert Frost in front of his writing cottage at his farm near Middlebury, Vermont. The farm has for many decades neighbored the Bread Loaf Writers' School, where Frost often taught and read his poetry.

strously ugly" house in Bridgewater, Connecticut (now handsomely restored and turned into a museum).

At the time, Anne and I had a summer home about twenty miles away in Washington, Connecticut, and we invited Brooks to meet us there. To be quite candid, the meeting was called so that Brooks could give Otto Bettmann the once-over. Brooks, of course, had every right and reason to be choosy. He was seventeen years older than I and considerably better known in the literary world.

To my pleasure, I passed with flying colors. A handsome man with a bristling moustache and brush-cut hair, Brooks was rather shy when meeting new acquaintances. But from the outset we hit it off well. He seemed impressed with our modest, antique-decorated home. A rapport between the wives—both assertive individuals—was more elusive. Brooks's second wife, Gladys, was a somewhat stentorian woman who seemed bent on scrutinizing every nook and cranny of our habitat (including the inside of the refrigerator).

Spouses aside, Brooks and I established a fine, productive working relationship that was enriched by the close proximity in which we lived and the agglomeration of like-minded artists and writers in our neighborhood. The New Milford–Woodbury–Bridgewater triangle was a haven of America's intellectual elite (such as Arthur Miller and William Styron) and remains so to this day.

Our Literary Heritage was completed over the course of a year. Once we hit our stride, Brooks left the graphic shaping of the book pretty much to me. (The page-spread headlines were developed from Brooks's evocative text. For example, of Melville he had written: "In his mind there loomed an early and tragic sense of life, with the sea a symbol of the enormity of evil.") In his introduction, Brooks paid me a high compliment: "As a cultivated newcomer, Dr. Bettmann approached my book with a kind of alert curiosity that is rare among native Americans . . . and he felt for my theme an enthusiasm that could be possible only in one discovering it for himself."

Our Literary Heritage became an alternate selection of the Book-of-the-Month Club. When I learned of this, I called Brooks excitedly to give him the news. Like so many writers, he was superb with words on paper but rather hesitant of speech—and he hated the phone. But strangely enough, he hardly seemed interested even in these good tidings—perhaps because he was more accustomed than I to such a yearned-for happy event. Our book was reprinted as a quality paperback. It even was translated into Arabic, of all things.

Though he was shy by nature, Brooks never avoided a fight—even taking on Adolf Hitler. When Hitler boasted that during his five-month imprisonment (1923–24) he had read a thousand books, Brooks pronounced this an absurd claim, commenting dryly that he had read all day long every day of his life and had been able to study and absorb no more than some five hundred titles.

Van Wyck Brooks and I remained friends until his death in 1963.

A pictorial history of music— the "divine art."

AS MY DAYS have been enriched with music since early childhood, it was only natural that I would eventually turn my bookmaking ambitions to that "divine art." Pictures of great composers and musical instruments I had long collected with a special abandon—*con amore*, so to speak. A history of music was a natural extension of that passion.

It would have been easiest simply to organize my musical picture file in chronological order and create a visual pageant of the subject, but albums of this sort were already on the market. My concept was different: I believed that the pictures and supporting text should be presented in a way that would help the reader comprehend the various styles of music that had evolved in the context of our developing civilization.

At that time the history of music that was most distinguished by its qualities of comprehensiveness and unified point of view was Paul Henry Lang's *Music in Western Civilization* (published by W. W. Norton in 1946). Its outlook and vigorous presentation made this book eminently suited to set the pattern for the pictorial book I

Above: "Fabbio Orsini from Naples, a good player of the great lute"—a musician in the papal orchestra immortalized in a sixteenth-century sketchbook. Right: "Brahms Fantasy"—from a series of evocative engravings by the German surrealist Max Klinger (1857–1920).

Conductor at the papal court as sketched by a sixteenth-century observer. The rolled score is the forerunner of today's baton.

I try my hand at publishing and produce a portable archive.

The founder pictorialized. Design by Friedman Studio.

envisioned. I was delighted to discover that Lang's interest in such a project matched my own, and we agreed to collaborate on making his history into a picture book. (Actually, Lang left the shaping of the book in my hands. I met him only once, over drinks at Schrafft's, during the book's incubation.)

As a special feature, I decided to interrupt the picture spreads of the book with "subject surveys" placed at logical intervals. For example, Lang's discussion of Domenico Scarlatti was complemented with a unit on the history of the harpsichord. In the Wagner chapter, we offered a pictorial survey on the growth of modern orchestras and the growing prominence of conductors. In keeping with the aesthetics of the subject, I tried to give the book a highly artistic stamp, introducing masterworks of art—some known, some newly discovered. Published in 1960, *A Pictorial History of Music* went through several reprintings and has remained popular among music lovers.

AFTER PUBLISHING FIVE BOOKS with other publishers, I couldn't rest until I started my own publishing house, be it only a miniature version. Picture House Press, the Archive's in-house publishing unit, would ultimately turn out but one volume, but it was a very profitable and satisfying venture.

In the early 1960s, I hatched a rather grandiose scheme: why not make the Archive itself the subject of a book? I decided to create an anthology of our most significant and usable pictures in each category, which would be called *The Bettmann Portable Archive*. The volume would serve both as a pictorial encyclopedia and as a catalog of what we had to offer. Unlike many catalogs, it would have a price tag: fifteen dollars (later upped to twenty-five dollars).

Before the *Portable Archive* was published, if an editor or artist needed a picture of an aardvark or the first zeppelin, we made up "approval shipments"—six to ten pictures on the subject from which the customer could choose. The *Portable Archive* put windows in our picture house, so to speak, by showing our subjects in small scale. Customers could order pictures by number right out of the catalog.

Designed by Herbert Migdoll (now a renowned ballet photographer), the book offered close to four thousand miniature illustrations, all arranged under topic headings from "Absurdities" to "Zoology." Each picture was indexed and cross-referenced. In addition, we developed what we called the Idea and Image Index. If an artist needed a picture to illustrate the idea of suspense, he was referred to a number

1. Monstrous Abduction.

2. Reader's Dust-Protector.　3. Learned Skeleton.　4. Man's Beauty Mask.　5. Heavyweight Bicyclist.　6. Lady's Neck-Stretcher.　7. Railroad Protection Garb.　8. Man-Bearing Tree.

9. King of the Albinos.　10. Pregnant, 1552.　11. Inseparable Twins.　12. Nailed Shoes in Perspective.　13. Weird Beard.　14. Toenail-Cutting Machine.　15. Abysmal Miscalculation.

Above: Typical example of a *Portable Archive* page. Each picture is referenced in a detailed subject index. Right: The *Portable Archive* displayed picture material covering a broad spectrum of moods and events. Below right: The Idea and Image Index helps art directors to dramatize headlines with old, often humorous graphics.

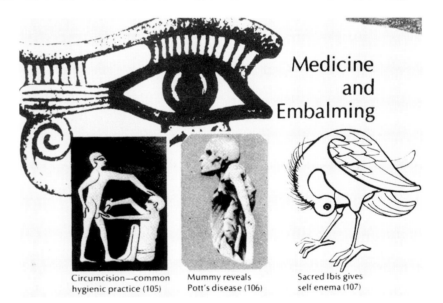

Medicine and Embalming

Circumcision—common hygienic practice (105)

Mummy reveals Pott's disease (106)

Sacred Ibis gives self enema (107)

Above left: An avid bookman since my early days, I took delight in supervising production of the *Portable Archive* with Ed Simmons, head of Chaucer Press. Above right: Discussing plans for the *Portable Archive* with Melvin Gray, my stepson and president of the Archive from 1974 to 1980. Mel and I made a good team: he was trained as an engineer and endowed with good business sense, while I was more academically inclined. Below right: A patient pachyderm is mounted by New York youngsters for a ride around Central Park. From the "Circus" section of the *Portable Archive*.

The heights of brutality: Druids—
Gaul's powerful priests—set fire to a
wooden colossus to sacrifice virgins
and punish evildoers. From a 1712
edition of Caesar's *De Bello Gallico*.
An example from the "Crime and
Punishment" section of the *Portable
Archive*.

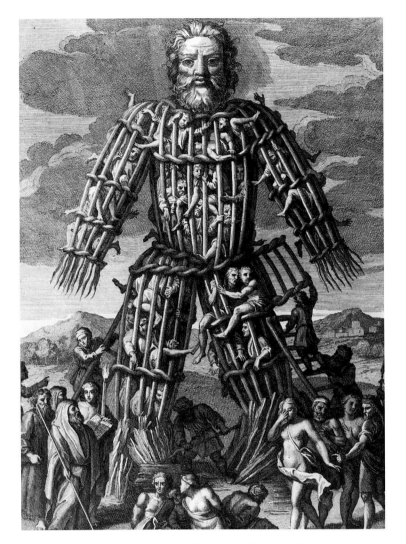

that showed a man hanging from a cliff. An editor who wanted to
express age might choose the picture of a cross section of a tree showing the yearly growth rings. Clients were able to draw inspiration in
absentia from our files and order by mail or phone rather than visit
the Archive in person—which helped to open an international market.

The Bettmann Portable Archive was a onetime venture that enabled
me—at least in a miniscule way—to play publisher, with all the accompanying thrills and chills. Its appearance in 1966 generated a
flurry of publicity. *American Artist* had this to say: "High fissionable
stuff. . . . Like the non-portable Archive, the Portable one shows the
masterful analytical eye, the profound selectivity, the rich humor of
Dr. Bettmann himself." For me the most memorable exposure was my
appearance on the *Today Show*, where I was interviewed by Hugh
Downs.

A new revised edition was published in 1992.

The Good Old Days debunks
nostalgia—I bite the hand that
has fed me.

A MAN WHO MAKES his living from pictures of the past and then sets out to author a book highly critical of nostalgia might seem like the fool who saws off the tree branch on which he is sitting. But that's just what I did. Paradoxical as it may seem, *The Good Old Days— They Were Terrible* was to become a highly successful book and no threat to the Bettmann Archive. It has even been used as supplementary reading in history courses. My irreverent approach to the past may have something to do with its perennial appeal.

Daily exposure to old pictures led me to the conviction that our nostalgia cult is overdone and obscures a candid appraisal of the present. The good old days were not as good as popular histories and novels often present them. We are inclined to see the past through

New York suffered from colossal traffic jams long before the advent of the automobile age. During "the good old days" of horse-drawn vehicles, it was said to take "more skill to cross Broadway than to cross the Atlantic in a clamboat."

Above left: Pittsburgh in 1880 was so beset by soot from the steel mills that it was said a man putting on a white shirt in the morning would find it blackened by noon. Above right: "The golf links lie so near the mill / That almost every day / The laboring children can look out / And watch the men at play."—Sarah Norcliffe Cleghorn (1915). Below right: A black man lynched for the alleged rape of a white woman in Beckley, West Virginia, ca. 1880.

A Victorian housewife succumbs before a demonically hot "patent stove."

rose-colored glasses, or, as John Simon of *New York Magazine* put it, "Whatever may have besmirched those lambent days is conveniently swept under the carpet of oblivion": the plight of workers, the exploitation of children, the cruel fate of the sick and the insane. The blood, sweat, and tears of the past have dried up. What remains is a picture of charm, ease, and good feeling, the illusion that the good old days were all fun—a continual flow of picnics and hayrides and Fourth of July celebrations. However, an 1857 *Harper's Monthly* reported: "Not in the lifetime of most men has there been so much grave and deep apprehension. . . . The domestic economic situation is in chaos. Our dollar is weak throughout the world. Prices are so high as to be utterly impossible. . . . Of our troubles, no man can see the end."

There is no doubt that today we confront overwhelming problems such as pollution, addiction, overpopulation, and crime; but in matters of health and well-being, we have advanced markedly. It has been said that the average worker of today, though not free of hardships, enjoys more of the good things of life—in food and fun—than did Henry VIII. To give just one example: the smoggy air of New York City today is still better than in 1910, when the poisonous puffy clouds of smokestacks were totally unregulated. (Today factories are banned from the city.) Add to this the deficiencies of the sewerage system, the lack of street-cleaning facilities, the nuisance of horse manure, and you can see why a visitor of the 1870s called New York a "nasal disaster." Nor should we forget the slums, the hospitals that were plague houses, and the fourteen-hour workday.

Technological progress often brings annoying side effects. Our problems today certainly can be discomforting, but we exacerbate them by hoping for instant solutions—in keeping with Bismarck's verdict that "the more civilized we get, the more we feel the gnaw of dissatisfaction." Thus, surrounded by abundance and miraculous inventions, we feel nostalgia for a less complicated life. *The Good Old Days—They Were Terrible* offered a corrective view of a period we tend to idealize, and by doing so perhaps it opened readers' eyes to the many blessings of our own time.

The book had another distinction: I sold the idea to a publisher without a hitch, practically over the telephone. This was a rare piece of good fortune when one considers how many outstanding books had to be peddled around and around before they were finally accepted. Flaubert once received a publisher's rejection slip that stated, "You have buried your novel under a heap of detail—utterly superfluous" (André Bernard, *Rotten Reviews* [1991], p. 27).

When the idea for *The Good Old Days* had crystallized I called Bob Loomis, executive editor of Random House and a man with an unfailing eye for winners. (He edited the two National Book Award winners of 1988: Peter Dexter's *Paris Trout* and Neil Sheehan's *A Bright Shining Lie*.) Loomis was intrigued by the idea, and soon the project was off and running. First published in August 1974, the book has gone through twenty-two printings and has sold 140,000 copies. Even the Japanese issued an annotated edition. Perhaps they too have had their fill of nostalgia.

A Word from the Wise combines quotes and images.

IT'S TIME FOR a little confession: I am not a particularly cheerful fellow. If there is a strain of hilarity in my makeup, it is heavily overlaid with Schopenhauerian pessimism. Still, an occasional streak of errant comic frivolity ripples my otherwise serious demeanor. Some have flattered me by saying that I have an infallible eye for the comic in the graphic arts. Indeed, I have been credited with the discovery of much laugh-provoking "believe-it-or-not" stuff—earning me the title of "grand master of graphic absurdities."

Casting about for a new project to tackle, I thought I might be able to combine the seriousness of Bettmann the wordman with the fey

Whilst Adam slept,
Eve from his side arose.
Strange—his first sleep
would be his last repose.
—Anonymous

"A committee is a gathering of men
who individually can do nothing,
but collectively can meet and decide
that nothing can be done."
—Josh Billings.

"Half of the modern drugs could
well be thrown out of the window,
except that the birds might eat
them."—Dr. Martin Henry Fischer.
Woodcut, ca. 1890.

"The society of women is the foundation of good manners."—Goethe.

spirit of Bettmann the picture man. The result was *A Word from the Wise,* imaginatively designed by Fred Czufin and published by Crown Publishers in 1977. I can perhaps best explain why I felt moved to produce this book by quoting from my own foreword.

Whatever it be—love or money, lox or medicine—you may be certain that someone, somewhere, has said something memorable on the subject. . . .

It is a fact that words and pictures work well together. One enhances the other. This I know from experience. As an obsessive picture sleuth from way back, I started with a cigar box of old photographs and wound up with an Archive of some three million pictures. And in a lifetime of reading, I have culled with equal avidity picturesque sayings and words of wisdom—from Socrates and Bach to James Baldwin and Gloria Steinem. To team up these pithy observations with amusing illustrations, I thought, might double the pleasure they could give.

This book is the result: an illustrated alphabet of quotations, a sampling of great thoughts combined with pictures from the Bettmann Archive. May they join in tandem to provide you with solace and guidance, an occasional uplift, or a wry smile—"a sufficiency to brighten your day."

Be silent as a politician,
for talking may beget suspicion.
—Jonathan Swift

IT WAS IN THE mid-1950s that I had first met Hans P. Kraus, New York's leading antiquarian bookman. He dealt with the world's most richly endowed libraries and museums—institutions blessed with budgets in the millions. His purchase in 1970 of an original Gutenberg Bible and the even older Constance missal set new records and made headlines the world over. Appropriately, it was a book that brought us together, a meeting that would later on lead to a momentous transition in my life.

By chance I had acquired at a book auction a sixteenth-century volume of fashion illustrations, *Diversarium Nationum Habitus*, with comments by the Italian writer Bertelli (published in Venice in 1592). After photographing some of the book's woodcut prints, I had no further use for this relatively valuable volume, so I hoped to sell it.

I called Kraus and asked if he would be interested in my purported treasure. He asked me to "bring it around." Kraus received me cordially and took me on a tour of his gilt-edged townhouse at 16 East Forty-sixth Street (the former abode of the Lehman family). The place was wood-paneled throughout, and the walls were lined with glass-fronted display cases containing luminescently beautiful reproductions of medieval manuscripts. The originals, with values running into the millions, were kept in a vault that would have done credit to a banking house.

Once settled in his studio, Kraus casually looked at the Bertelli volume. I could see he was not much impressed with my imagined "treasure." It was decidedly "small potatoes" for a man who at times had outbid at auctions the supercapitalist J. P. Morgan. "No," he said

Below left: H. P. Kraus displays the *St. Alban's Apocalypse*, which he bought in 1959 for $182,000, setting a new record for bibliophilic rarities. Below right: An illustration from *Diversarium Nationum Habitus* (1592), a rare book on Renaissance fashions that I hoped to sell to H. P. Kraus. Instead he asked me if I would be willing to sell him the Bettmann Archive.

firmly, handing me back my book. "No, I am not interested in this. But since you are here, would you consider selling me the Bettmann Archive?"

I was quite floored by the directness of his totally unexpected offer. But it didn't take me long to recover. Since I was only in my mid-fifties, and things were rolling along smoothly, I told Kraus politely that I saw no need for such a transaction at present. Though neither of us had struck a deal, we parted as friends.

Bowing out gracefully, I sell the Archive to the Kraus–Thomson conglomerate.

BUT TIMES CHANGE and so do we. By the late 1970s, approaching the biblical "three-score and ten," the years had crept up on me, though I was still well and in full command of my operation. Nevertheless, one cannot carry on forever, and I had no desire to die with my boots on, or on a pile of old photographs. I concluded that it was better to sell the Archive while things were still going well, rather than being compelled by some misfortune to bail out and thus lose in the process.

In the late 1970s mergers were all the rage. Companies paired up left and right; small firms were gobbled up by large ones—some of the latter getting a good case of indigestion in the process. But some small businessmen who sold their stake became millionaires overnight. In the course of such pipe dreams, I recalled my encounter with Kraus almost two decades earlier, remembering the interest he had expressed in the Archive.

Since our earlier meeting, Kraus's enterprise had gone through an impressive expansion. Originally confined to the field of rare books, H. P. Kraus had joined forces with the Thomson family's Canadian newspaper empire to form the worldwide publishing and reprint corporation of Kraus–Thomson. (Kraus eventually bought out Thomson in 1988 to form the independent publishing conglomerate Kraus Organization Limited.) Thus, when I began to contemplate the sale of the Archive, I decided to drop a note to Kraus, or rather to the Kraus–Thomson corporate headquarters, telling them that I would now consider joining their ranks.

As a rule, prospective mergers are fraught with long, drawn-out negotiations, offers, counteroffers, and at times downright phony ploys. To my surprise, I was promptly informed that Kraus–Thomson would indeed entertain the thought of including the Bettmann Archive in its expansion plans. In fact, our jointure was to be formed at the price of a postage stamp and in the friendliest of spirits.

The last meeting with the Kraus high command took place in our Boca Raton winter home in November 1980; it was there that we reached a final settlement. I say "we" because my wife, Anne, played a crucial role in the negotiations. Sensing my nervousness, she warned me that "this is not the way to approach a chess game." Anne also politely swayed Kraus's president Herb Gstalder and vice president and treasurer Bernard Tager to raise their ante a bit. All was resolved pleasantly. Herb closed the discussion with the joking suggestion, "Mrs. Bettmann, would you like to work for us?"

The news that I was selling the Archive was met with surprise, even regret. My stepson Wendell responded: "Bettmann without pictures? Why, you will feel like Rubenstein without a piano or Babe Ruth without a bat!" In a nostalgic article "From Freud to Bicycling Monks," *Time* commented on my departure as a fixture in the publishing field. My colleagues in the picture agency field also seemed to feel a sense of betrayal—as if their esteemed colleague had deserted his ship. Indeed, I was gently chided by the daughter of my friendly competitor Jay Culver. Harriet had succeeded her father in the management of his agency. "How could you do it?" she asked me. "Culver Pictures will never be for sale."

The Bettmann Archive prospers under the new aegis.

FAR FROM REGRETTING giving up my reins at the Archive, I welcomed its sale as the realization of a dream I had long entertained. I had always hoped to create a comprehensive picture service, covering human history from earliest times to the latest news event.

By aligning the Bettmann Archive with Kraus–Thomson—followed by the latter's association with United Press International, Reuters, and Hulton (the BBC's picture archive)—this full coverage of history has now been achieved. Current photos by the hundreds arrive every day to be distributed to the press, then cataloged for permanent use and safekeeping. Picture seekers no longer have to consult a multiplicity of sources to fill their graphic needs; all can be satisfied in one well-organized picture emporium of more than twelve million images—an enterprise that runs twenty-four hours a day, seven days a week.

It was several years before the entire operation was brought together in one location. But on November 8, 1989, I was invited to the grand opening of a new and expanding facility at 902 Broadway, in New York's Flatiron district.

My thoughts drifted back to my first darkroom, the clothes closet in my modest flat on West Forty-fourth Street. The struggling, one-man operation had mushroomed into a bustling modern emporium, staffed by sixty bright-faced, mostly young researchers and technicians using the latest computer and communication technology for all manner of pictorial reproduction and research.

From all appearances and to the "founder's" genuine delight, the Bettmann Archive without Bettmann has done exceedingly well. But how did Bettmann fare without the Archive?

Right: Final signing of the Bettmann-Kraus purchase contract on January 8, 1981. Looking on are Melvin Gray (left), president of the Bettmann Archive, and Herbert Gstalder (right), head of the Kraus-Thomson publishing group. Far right: David Greenstein, a former Fulbright scholar and professor of English at Middlebury College, now heads the Bettmann operation. Below: The new headquarters of the Archive—now named simply "Bettmann"—at 902 Broadway, New York City. Photo by Katherine G. Bang.

A sampling of the millions of classic shots now available from BETTMANN, which incorporates the UPI and Reuters picture libraries.

Above: The sensational news shot that shows the giant *Hindenburg* zeppelin crashing to the earth in flames, just as it was about to be moored to its mast at Lakehurst, New Jersey, on May 6, 1937. Right: President Ronald Reagan engages in good-natured banter during the White House News Photographers Association dinner, May 8, 1983. Opposite page, bottom: Harry Truman triumphantly holds up a copy of the *Chicago Tribune* that pronounced his adversary, Thomas E. Dewey, the winner in the 1948 presidential election—a memorable gaffe in newspaper history.

Left: Dr. Robert Oppenheimer, banned from the Atomic Energy Commission as a security risk, shown during a lecture at the Institute for Advanced Study in Princeton, New Jersey, June 1954. Right: The famous publicity shot of Marilyn Monroe holding down her billowing skirt as she posed over a subway grating. It was used to promote her hit comedy film, *The Seven Year Itch* (1954).

Top: The sea, the sea. The view from the terrace of my oceanfront apartment in Boca Raton. Bottom: Entrance to the main campus of Florida Atlantic University at Boca Raton. From its modest beginnings in 1965, this institution has grown to accommodate over thirteen thousand students, including two affiliated campuses at Fort Lauderdale and Davie. Under the leadership of its president Anthony Catanese, a third full-scale teaching center is being planned near Palm Beach.

6  GO SOUTH,

OLD MAN

AFTER THE ARCHIVE was sold, Anne and I decided to fold up our tent and leave New York for good. I must say Anne had rigged up a pleasant "tent" on Sutton Place South—a far cry from the railroad flat on Fifty-seventh Street (in environment though not in distance) where we had begun the first major expansion of the Archive. We were well prepared to face the retirement quandary of where to go and what to do: since 1975 we had spent the winters in Florida, and we were ready to make the state our permanent home. Professionally, I had no particular fear of the void of unemployment because I had already established a firm connection with Florida Atlantic University during our winter sojourns in Boca Raton. How we ended up in this oddly named town (in Spanish, "mouth of the rat") is in itself a saga marked by fortuitous coincidences.

While I was still working full-time at the Archive and enjoying New York's amenities, I didn't even want to hear about Florida as a permanent habitat. It has been said of ingrained New Yorkers (such as myself) that they know their town is an absurd place to live in but that—in a perverse sense—they consider this absurdity to be one of its delights. We could hardly picture ourselves living anywhere but in New York—or perhaps New England, Anne's original home. And we were well aware that Henry James (though long ago) and others had considered Florida a "cultural Sahara," with nothing more interesting to offer than "grapefruits and oranges."

How times have changed. Today, Florida's Gold Coast is witness to a most impressive cultural ground swell—competing at times with the best New York has to offer in music, dance, and the fine arts. The sun still shines year-round in South Florida, but the area by no means attracts only the old and the infirm. The young and ambitious are also heavily represented among the new arrivals—seeking employment in the corporate headquarters or expanding research facilities of firms like IBM, Siemens, Sony, and W. R. Grace.

Once we decided to seek a winter home in South Florida, the choice of a community in which to settle was made by me in typical book-man fashion: I consulted the *American Library Directory* and discovered a listing for a little town in Palm Beach County of which I had been only faintly aware—Boca Raton. Its university, I learned, had a library of 280,000 volumes. A good library always has been essential for me—like water for a fish. It was a stroke of good fortune that I was to become attached to the Florida Atlantic University library, with superb research facilities at my command.

Before our arrival in Boca Raton, Anne and I—essentially New Englanders in taste—wondered how we would fare among the "wicker set." With our eighteenth-century antiques, could we properly adjust to the casual, semitropical Florida life-style? We decided to bring most of our belonging anyway, and Anne once again applied her magic touch to create a haven at the Stratford Arms, an oceanfront condominium complex. Our antiques dominated our twentieth-floor apartment, but we added a modern touch to the ambience with our collection of paintings of the New York school—an unorthodox combination that enabled us to live happily in Florida "the New England way."

Mr. Harper's horse and me: brothers under the skin?

DURING OUR FIRST winter vacation in 1975, a question began to gnaw on my mind: what should I—incurable workaholic that I am—do with my free time? Should I pound the pavement looking for employment at the ripe old age of seventy-three? "Quit, already!" was the reaction of my friends, but alas, I am simply not cut out to do nothing. A busybody incarnate, I subscribe to the doctrine that one should keep occupied "as long as there is a body." I am reminded of another obsessive worker (of the equine species), also laboring in the

"field" of publishing: the legendary Harper's horse. One hundred years after his retirement, the horse's story was told in a 1952 advertisement for the Home Insurance Company.

This horse had spent most of its life trudging in a tight circle, turning a vertical shaft to power the printing presses of Harper Brothers publishing house. From seven in the morning until noon, and from one o'clock until six in the evening when the final whistle sounded, the horse tromped dutifully in his circular path. After twenty years had passed, Mr. Harper felt his helper had done enough, and he retired his horse to roam freely on the Harper farm in New Jersey. One morning Harper observed that as a whistle sounded at a nearby factory, the horse trotted out to the middle of the pasture, where he trudged in a circle around a tree until the factory whistle blew at night. Every day until he died, Harper's horse hobbled along, making his rounds. Such is the force of habit developed in a lifetime of work.

I have always felt a kinship to my quadrupedal colleague. No sooner had we settled in Florida than I felt the compulsion to go round and round until the whistle blew. But where could I find a place "to tromp"?

An academic interlude offers a taste of the life I might have lived.

GUIDED BY SOME homing instinct, I made haste to visit the seven-hundred-acre campus of Florida Atlantic University, the institution whose library had led me to Boca Raton. I was immediately impressed by its expanse and bustling crowds of students. I began by paying a call on the Department of History. Its chairman, Dr. Donald Curl, greeted me cordially as a fellow worker in the field. My reception in the school's Department of Learning Resources was equally friendly. Its facilities in photography, graphic arts, and television production—all fields in which I had been involved in New York—were exceptional. I had the comfortable feeling that, late as it was in my life, I would fit in here somewhere and indulge my penchant for picture research. Hank Schubert, who at the time headed Learning Resources, warmly welcomed a New York graphics man. He offered me an office in his department, where I could pursue my interests as I saw fit. What a happy landing in a part of the country I had once so arrogantly disparaged!

Each winter, I strengthened my ties with FAU—formalizing them in the fall of 1978. Still a part-time Floridian, I was appointed adjunct professor of history and given an office in the Humanities Building. It

Receiving the degree of doctor of humane letters at FAU commencement ceremonies on August 11, 1981.

was an ideal stomping ground for me, with the departments of philosophy, linguistics, and English nearby. A friendly and fruitful rapport developed between me and my newfound colleagues. How delightful to go next door to Dr. Boyd Breslow's office and engage in a discourse on medieval cathedrals, or to run over to Dr. Robert Schwarz, chairman of the philosophy department, to seek enlightenment on the pragmatism of William James. All this was a most welcome change for a semiretired businessman who had always yearned for the thinker's world of academia.

Dr. Curl put me under no obligation to lecture. When I confessed to him that I felt quite uneasy about my lack of a formal assignment, he graciously reassured me: "You don't have to do anything—just be here." However, I felt I could make a contribution to the university's academic program. For the winter term 1979–80, I scheduled a lecture course on pictorial history and research. I practiced the visual gospel I intended to preach by supporting my discussions with a vast array of slides.

The three-hour weekly course attracted a lively group—prospective journalists, librarians, and filmmakers, as well as would-be historians. We discussed picture sources, filing systems, and copyright and tried to find answers to the perennial question, "What's a good picture?" During our sessions someone would inevitably bring up the familiar cliché that "one picture is worth a thousand words"—a tired old chestnut that was fervently believed by my television-age students.

Taking up the gauntlet, I admonished the class to look critically at this old saw. While teaching pictorialism, I still was eager to apprise my students of the rich tradition of cultural literacy too often neglected in today's curriculum. As a picture man by profession but a word man by inclination, I always tried to convince my students to balance their enthusiasm for the graphic with an awareness of the power of words. I cited a *Saturday Review* editorial by Norman Cousins:

Some say nothing is more memorable than a picture. We disagree. No visual image is as vivid as the image created by the mind in response to words. There is more to life than meets the eye. The ability of words to throw a loop around human personalities, to penetrate the inner space of character, is exceeded by nothing that can be given visual form.

But it seems that a generation gap yawned between me and my young students, who were caught up in a high-tech, image-saturated world. The class did not go for my literary theories, though our discussions were held in the friendliest of spirits (my comic art slides often creating gales of laughter). Inevitably I got my comeuppance. When I came to our last class I found a message on the blackboard scrawled in big letters: "A good picture is worth a thousand bucks."

Although subsequent publishing commitments precluded my teaching this course again, the university acknowledged my humble efforts by conferring on me in the summer of 1981 the honorary degree of doctor of humane letters. Still, I was not to be idle: other assignments materialized to tantalize me. They appeared out of the blue and provided the unexpected excitement necessary to keep me on the *qui vive*.

Immortalized on celluloid with Dudley Moore in Lovesick.

H O W C O U L D I in my wildest dreams have imagined that after a life spent as the picture man I would be called on to play a role in a popular motion picture?

The Ladd Company called me in Florida early in the fall of 1981 with an invitation to join the cast of its forthcoming film *Lovesick*, starring Dudley Moore. With actors of ancient vintage in oversupply, I couldn't imagine why the director, Marshall Brickman, might want me. But the prospect of putting in my bid for immortality in the flickering arts was irresistible.

Brickman had seen my photo in a *New York Times Magazine* article, "The Bettmann Behind the Archive" (October 18, 1981), and he felt I bore a striking resemblance to Sigmund Freud, whose psychoanalytic theories were being spoofed in the movie. In view of my lack of thespian experience, it was fortunate that Brickman did not want me for the role of Freud himself (that part went to Alec Guinness), but rather for the role of Dr. Morris Waxmann—a nagging, nearly senile psychoanalyst from Freud's Vienna circle. I was relieved to hear that the role was to be merely a comic cameo.

"How comic?" my always-protective wife demanded to know—fearing that the role being offered would be that of a dithering old-timer. Before I signed a contract, she requested a copy of the script. Sure enough, it required that I stagger on the scene and blurt out, "Where's the bathroom?" With Anne's protective input, the line was

Portraying an aged psychoanalyst in the movie comedy *Lovesick,* I reprimanded Dudley Moore for sleeping with his patient.

eliminated and the script toned down. But I was still concerned about my big-screen impression, brief as it was designed to be.

"You must remember," Brickman consoled me, "that time on screen is not necessarily equated with the amount of dialogue. Your presence will be felt more significantly than the dialogue would seem to indicate." This settled, I flew to New York and was put up at the St. Regis Hotel at the Ladd Company's expense. Every morning at 6:45 on the dot, I climbed into a company limousine and settled back to contemplate, with mounting excitement, my screen debut.

The dinner scene in which I was to appear was filmed in a fashionable West Side apartment and took a week to shoot. Dudley Moore played a psychoanalyst who had become sexually involved with a beautiful young woman patient (Elizabeth McGovern)—a moral transgression of the first degree against the psychoanalyst's professional code. I was part of the committee threatening Moore with expulsion from the psychoanalytic fraternity. My fellow doctors were played by John Huston, Alan King, Stefan Schnabel, and Selma Diamond. (I spent delightful luncheon hours with Stefan, listening to his stories about his father, the famed piano virtuoso Artur Schnabel.)

My immortal lines—"Did you have sexual relations on the couch?" and "Have some corn . . . or are you afraid of roughage?"—were shot and reshot endlessly. I marveled at the patience of Marshall Brickman and the crew. Even more patience was required when Dudley Moore was called upon to perform the old magic trick of whisking off the tablecloth from a table lavishly set for dinner, leaving the plates and silverware safely in place.

Other memorable moments included playing some Schubert, four-hand, with Dudley Moore, who is quite an accomplished pianist. John Huston and I exchanged notes about primitive art while we were supposed to be engaged in "lively discussion" in front of the camera. He told me that he considered his film on Sigmund Freud to be his greatest intellectual (though perhaps not filmic) accomplishment.

When *Lovesick* was finally shown in theaters, my on-screen time had been cut to about five minutes. There were long-term benefits, however. I became a member of the Screen Actors Guild, entitled to dental care (not mental care, which I may need more) as long as I remained a Guild member. Moreover, the Guild's retirement fund credited my account in the amount of $189.79, which would be available to me after ten years of continued membership. So why worry about the future?

When my friend Robert Loomis of Random House saw a preview of *Lovesick,* he wrote me: "At first I had some doubts that it could really be Otto, but when you opened your mouth I almost fell out of my chair." Since the film is still available in a cassette version, many of my friends have seen my debut (and final) performance and felt likewise.

A big bite: trying to put the entire history of the world between covers.

FROM MY MODEST BEGINNINGS as an author, my subjects had grown in scope with each new book. Perhaps it was inevitable that given the opportunity I would be presumptuous enough to undertake no less than a pictorial history of the world, using the full resources of the Bettmann Archive. Such a project was indeed to take shape soon after *The Good Old Days* was published in 1974 under the Random House imprint. Pleased with this earlier book's success, this publisher was again ready to back me.

I had already established the structure of the book when we began wintering in Florida in 1975. It was fortunate that I had a capable deputy on the project, my stepdaughter Beverly's husband, Manley Stolzman. A former assistant to public relations wizard Edward Bernays, Manley stepped into the breach and assumed the book's

Glenwood I. Creech, former president of Florida Atlantic University, inspects a dedication copy of my pictorial world history.

coeditorship. *The Bettmann Archive Picture History of the World* appeared in 1978 to some praise, but it also suffered some harsh criticism.

Vogue magazine adjudged the book "fabulous." However, Eliot Clermont Smith, book editor of the *Village Voice,* flayed me mercilessly for too-small reproduction of the pictures. ("Does Random House hate Bettmann?" the review asked.) But the history of the world—from caveman to man in space—required more than three thousand pictures organized into comprehensible page layouts. How were we to accommodate them all without photo reduction? Book pages are not made of rubber—at least not yet.

Members of the advertising fraternity looked at the volume, so rich in pictorial lore, as a bonanza. Henry Wolf, a leading New York art director and photographer, observed: "Anybody who works with pictures must have it."

The Picture History of the World involved an incredible amount of planning and work—but then, all books do. Books are, after all, like children: both begin with such great parental/authorial hopes, which are rarely fulfilled. As Goethe said, "If all children lived up to our hopes, we would have a world populated with geniuses." Correspondingly, authors always yearn for the best-seller list. Few make it.

We were to have yet another disappointment: the big event that we hoped would bring *The Picture History of the World* to national attention was not destined to be. Tom Brokaw had discussed the book

A picture unit covering World War I —illustrating the synoptic treatment featured throughout the book.

The pictorial history offered conclusions both optimistic (novelist Thomas Mann: "The history of the world is a record of progress—even when all signs point to the contrary") and pessimistic (sexologist Auguste Henri Forel: "World history is a succession of messes").

HOPES AND FEARS are strangely intermingled as the age of technocracy remodels our world. We are witnessing unprecedented accomplishments and are called upon at the same time to solve unprecedented problems. Progress always creates new troubles to plague mankind: medical miracles with all their benefits have brought us face to face with the problems of the population explosion and the vicissitudes of aging. Technological advances force us to adjust to a new man-made environment; to cope with an unnatural acceleration in the pace of life. And over all our technical breakthroughs there hovers the specter of nuclear war.

Still, there is no reason for despair. Man the problem-solver, seen in historical perspective, has a triumphant record on the whole. If our problems today are enormous in scale, so are our resources to solve them. This thought must strengthen our resolve to face the future without fear. As Faulkner said in his famed Nobel Prize speech: "The basest thing of all is to be afraid. I believe man will not only endure, he will prevail."

with me in a videotaped interview for NBC's *Today Show*. The interview had gone well, I thought, and it was scheduled for broadcast on Thanksgiving Day, 1978. The endpapers of the book had been enlarged to wall size, to provide a dramatic backdrop for our discussion. Alas, the scheduled airdate was the same day the Reverend Jim Jones and his community of nine hundred followers committed mass suicide in Guyana. Needless to say, this event was hotter news than Bettmann's world history, and my interview was bumped off the air.

Though the world history wasn't as successful as some of my other ventures, I still think it had a valid plan and a hopeful message, in a spirit akin to Thomas Mann's observation: "The history of the world is a record of progress—even when all signs point to the contrary."

A Washington book celebration launches The Delights of Reading.

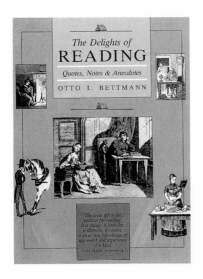

THOUGH I THOUGHT I had said a fond farewell to the publishing world when I sold the Archive in 1981, I found myself once again immersed in bookmaking—this time in the more leisurely, less literary climate of Florida. The little boy—over eighty years old by then—just couldn't keep his fingers out of the cookie jar. The project that was to occupy me next represented a return to my beginnings and a summing up of my previous avocations.

I have always been a voracious reader and an equally dedicated collector of pictures of people in the act of reading (a pastime that played a major part in sparking the idea of the Bettmann Archive). My quotation files and wordbooks, assembled over a lifetime, teemed with wise observations on reading—its benefits and dangers, pleasures and perils. It occurred to me that these elements could be fused to make a book about the joys of reading.

There was even the prospect of a tie-in with a budding organization that had been founded at the Library of Congress—the Center for the

The Delights of Reading was published for the benefit of the Center for the Book at the Library of Congress. Here I examine the book with John Cole, director of the Center.

The world of libraries exerts its perennial lure.

Book. The first branch of this organization was located not far from my Boca Raton home, at the Broward County Main Library in Fort Lauderdale. This local group was headed by Jean Trebbie, hostess of the television program *Book Beat* and a person of great charm and energy. When I broached the idea of the book to John Cole, national director of the Center, he encouraged me to proceed. I arranged that all royalties would be transferred to the Center for the Book—a small token of gratitude for the benefits I had derived from the pictorial largess of the Library of Congress.

The Delights of Reading appeared in November 1987 and was launched at a memorable gathering at the Library of Congress. The press gave a fine send-off to the slim, well-designed volume, which was published by David Godine of Boston. William Robertson, book editor of the *Miami Herald,* commented: "I intended to buy several copies of *The Delights of Reading.* Most will be sent to friends, but I am going to keep a couple for myself. The copy I have is less than a week old, and already it is dog-eared."

WHILE I HAD NO official connection with Florida Atlantic University as I was finishing *The Bettmann Archive Picture History of the World,* the FAU Wimberly Library remained my daily beat. Much was happening at this place—most notably the completion of a magnificent annex that would accommodate 800,000 additional volumes and state-of-the-art computer facilities.

When the major expansion and computerization of the library was completed in June 1986, the library's director, Harry Skallerup, suggested that I establish myself as a research associate in the Department of Special Collections. The backlog of rare and limited editions accumulated in this section needed organizing—a particularly appropriate assignment for me. Harry welcomed me with a letter that reflects his warmhearted nature. "I would like to put up a sign that I saw in a saloon many years ago," he wrote. "The sign read, 'Everyone brings happiness here. Some by coming in, and others by leaving.' Needless to say you are in the forefront of the first group."

The quarters assigned to me in the FAU Library were to become truly a bookman's haven, lined by shelves and shelves of fine editions, the dust of rare old volumes in the air. The adjoining office—the Department of Systems Development—serves as a receiving station for the latest books. The influx of new publications keeps me posted on what is happening today in the world of books, while—in my own

Left: A reader returns a giant tome to the Bibliothèque Nationale, Paris, ca. 1840. Right: America's most venerated reader, Abraham Lincoln, with his beloved son, Tad, in 1864. This famous portrait—based on a photograph by Matthew Brady—is from the Library of Congress Division of Prints and Photographs.

domain—I hold sway over the past. I feel like a kid in a candy shop. My activities now have the support of Dr. William Miller, since 1988 the director of FAU Libraries and Learning Resources, who is ably guiding the institution into the computer age.

Over the years, my office has become my professional home and the locus of displays of newfound treasures. Indeed, shortly after I took up my post, I made a fortuitous discovery among the Rare Book Room's folio volumes.

Major find of Confederate memorabilia makes national news.

WHEN I TOOK CHARGE of Rare Books, it was common knowledge that the department had in its safekeeping four leather-bound folios marked "C.S.A." Examining their contents more closely, I discovered that the volumes contained original manuscripts, letters, and mementos of Confederate leaders—among them original letters by Robert E. Lee, Jefferson Davis, Alexander Stephens, Judah P. Benjamin (the attorney general of the Confederacy and one of the most prominent Jews of nineteenth-century America). The pièce de résistance was a sampling of cloth clipped from the uniform of the dying Stonewall Jackson and a letter from a physician attending the general during his last days before he succumbed to blood poisoning after the amputation of his left arm.

I displayed the Confederate materials in an exhibit and compiled an annotated catalog. The display was enthusiastically welcomed by both

Above left: Pre–Civil War autograph of Judah P. Benjamin (September 18, 1856). Benjamin, a Jew born in St. Thomas, became secretary of state of the Confederacy. The postscript refers to the 1856 presidential election campaign of James Buchanan and his running mate, John C. Breckenridge. Above right: A Confederate songbook cover. Right: Autograph of John Hay (1838–1905), who had been the assistant to Lincoln's private secretary, John Nicolay, during the Civil War. Later secretary of state, Hay is shown at far right with Nicolay (left) and Lincoln. Hay and Nicolay coauthored the ten-volume *Life of Lincoln* (1891). Below: Document permitting the bearer to pass through Union lines at Harper's Ferry—scene of John Brown's raid on a federal arsenal in 1859.

One of the items in the Davis Music Collection—a pen sketch of Beethoven drawn from life by Moritz von Schwind, a German Romantic painter.

FAU students and a host of local Civil War buffs. But the find also gained national attention. Shelby Foote, the historian who was prominently featured in the stirring 1990 PBS *Civil War* series, called the find "tremendous." Herman Herst, a nationally known philatelist and manuscript expert based in Boca Raton, appraised our find's value at over one hundred thousand dollars.

Even though I consider myself a full-fledged American, I still wonder at our country's insatiable, never-flagging interest in the Civil War. The conflict has remained a national trauma exemplifying endurance and human greatness, but its wounds seem never to stop bleeding. This fascination with the Civil War is a unique phenomenon, but it is a tradition and a continuing fixation of the American mind that I cannot totally share because I am foreign-born.

National press coverage of our discovery helped us to solve the mystery of how we acquired the four C.S.A. volumes in the first place. *The Blue and the Gray,* the official organ of Civil War collectors, wrote: "The donor of this invaluable lode was not on record. But as soon as national publicity broke, he surfaced. It was James Cross, who had given the volumes to the university some fifteen years ago upon the death of his father, Eliot Cross, an avid collector of Civil War documents." Among all the treasures of the Rare Book Room—the whole of world literature in the finest illustrated editions—nothing exerts the pull of our Civil War Collection.

Another fine selection of rarities that came under my curatorship was donated to the university in 1987 by the English collectors Gillian and Richard E. Davis. The gift included a series of original editions of all nine of Beethoven's symphonies, as well as a valuable collection of the works of the Austrian composer Johann Nepomuk Hummel.

"If Bach is not in heaven, I'm not going."—William F. Buckley.

IT SHOULD BE CLEAR by now that very nearly every topic that has fascinated or delighted me for a considerable portion of my long life has ended up as the subject of another Bettmann book. Thus, it is only logical that I should have contemplated—and intermittently worked on—a new kind of Bach biography. When I broached this idea to a prominent music editor, she replied that there were already enough books on "stolid Bach." She didn't realize it isn't Bach who is stolid but the dull academic treatises about him. In my view, Bach was a live wire of inexhaustible vitality. I had hoped to do more than simply retell Bach's life in the usual chronological order or to produce yet another analysis of his works (the most frequent subject of books

In 1747 Bach visited Frederick the
Great, king of Prussia. A music-lover
and accomplished flutist, the "en-
lightened despot" had composed a
"royal theme" which Bach later developed into *The Musical Offering*.

about Bach). Rather, I envisioned a "psychobiography" that would
explore Bach's mind, his thoughts, his feelings, his working methods.
In the course of this pursuit I assembled a considerable Bach library
and developed what I call a "Bach Organon"—a file with hundreds of
subject entries allowing me to analyze Bach's life under such headings
as Applause, Businessman, Conductor, Father, Letter Writer, Mathe-
matician, and many other topics.

While I have derived much inspiration from this study, I had to
conclude as the years passed that undertaking a Bach biography is too
enormous a task for a man of my vintage. I also felt a certain kinship
to the hero of Bernard Malamud's *Dubin's Lives*, who gives up his
plan to write a biography of D. H. Lawrence because he comes to feel
like "an ant trying to fell an oak tree."

Lowering my sights, I have instead tried to develop several more
limited themes in the Bachian saga. One of my essays—"Bach and
Rhetoric"—was published in the *American Scholar* (Winter 1988).
This article offers a theory about the basis of Bach's music, the univer-

sal attraction it exerts, and the mystic sway it holds for its aficionados—summarized by the observation that "his music sets in order what life cannot." It also suggests that Bach's dominant creative form, the fugue, is a musical simile of life—not as it is, but as it should be. In the fugue, the interacting voices move up and down the scale to arrive after endless involutions at a harmonious finale—a powerful restatement of the original theme. This interplay of voices can be considered a metaphor of the multifarious encounters we have in life. In real life these encounters are not always happily resolved, but in Bach's music they are. Bach consolingly mends all the apparent disharmonies and brings us safely home.

This interpretation of the phenomenon of Bach appealed to Donal Henehan, then the music critic of the *New York Times,* who commented favorably on my thesis in his article "Sonorities Alone Do Not Suffice" (November 24, 1985).

An enriching friendship wrought by Johann Sebastian Bach.

THERE IS A MYSTERIOUS effluvium in Bach's music that makes all who love him kin. An earlier essay of mine in the *American Scholar,* "Bach at Potsdam" (Winter 1982), seems proof of this. It opened up for me a source of unexpected enrichment. A fellow Bach lover, Dr. Dianne Skafte (then a psychotherapist and family counselor based in Boulder, Colorado), wrote to me that she had read my article and was moved by the warmth of my presentation.

I could not help but acknowledge this gracious response, and ever since we have enjoyed a correspondence about Bach and everything else between heaven and earth. Ten years have not dimmed the joy of this magical encounter.

From her early letters and the poignancy of her observations, I pictured Dianne to be comfortably middle-aged. When she visited

Right: Relaxing at my Yamaha keyboard—a late-in-life dividend of my early musical training. Illustration for an article in *Boca Raton Magazine* (January 1988). Far right: A most rewarding Bachian friendship: I team up with Dr. Dianne Skafte to play one of the master's concertos for two pianos.

Florida for the first time, I was struck by her youth and beauty; her hair was fastened primly in a bun (something that appeals to the displaced Victorian that I am). I couldn't quite imagine this attractive young woman to be the Dianne Skafte of our correspondence. "Did your mother send you?" I blurted out.

She laughed endearingly, and our mutual rapport was instant. Though we live thousands of miles apart, a corpus of ideas, convictions, and mutually shared feelings has drawn us together in a warm Bachian friendship.

A companion in solitude.

THOUGH I HAVE BEEN blessed with a loving family and many friends, Bach's music palliates that existential loneliness that lies deep within each human soul. So long as I can move my fingers to play a little of his music, loneliness has little chance to creep up on me.

Every morning I begin with exercises performed to Bachian music. There is nothing more suited to doing one's push-ups than the assertive sound of Bach. His decisive rhythms are bracing, chasing away the brain's nocturnal shadows. No less a man than Pablo Casals followed a similar regimen—though less athletically oriented. In his Casals biography (p. 18), Albert Kahn recalls the master cellist's remarks: "In the past eighty years I have started each day in the same manner: I go to the piano and play two preludes and fugues by Bach . . . it is a sort of benediction of the house . . . a benediction of the world which I enjoy being a part of."

At the end of the day, I again take refuge in the unfathomable works of my patron saint. I sit down at the piano—or rather, my little earphone-quipped Yamaha, which I acquired to spare my neighbors. I reach on top of the pile of music for *The Well-Tempered Clavier.* "Well tempered" indeed is the music of Bach: running the gamut from sunlit contemplation and joy to sorrow and melancholy borne by a heroic heart. I turn to the tattered pages and tackle once more a prelude or a fugue on which I have worked for months (sometimes for a lifetime). As I immerse myself in these crystalline, logical structures, I leave for a few precious moments the disorderly world with its myriad unsolved problems and enter one where serenity and order prevail.

Bach always "takes me home." Conflicting thoughts that beset me during the day seem to fall in line. The rhythmic certainties, the sense of destination that prevails in all he wrote, prove infinitely bracing. And so to bed, perchance to dream.

Confessions of a workaholic.

I MUST CONFESS THAT my life has been filled to the brim with work. This is not an entirely laudable state, but one that fate has imposed on me. Double jeopardy has made me a workaholic. As a Jew in Germany, I had to hustle to prove myself. As a German in America, with pockets empty, I had to start all over again.

My obsessive working habits do not make me an ideal employer. The three-hour lunch and the extended coffee break are not for me. Mortimer Roane, a co-worker in my early days, once called me a "good-hearted slave driver." I demand much from myself, and hence from others. An impatient taskmaster, I subscribe to the French saying "Patience is the virtue of fools." (As must be obvious by now, "quotitis" is another of my eccentricities—for which I humbly apologize.)

But as for my workaholism, some rather smart men and women are in my pew—among them Ben Franklin, who admonished: "Does thou love life? Then do not squander time, for it is the stuff life is made of." Georgia O'Keeffe noted that many young artists had written to her asking for a prescription for success. She had a succinct answer for them: "Go home and work"—echoing the truth of the Roman saying *Labore omnia vincit*. And all of us—old and young alike—should remember Freud's observation that mental health is best assured by work and love. (Perhaps a reversal of the two is in order.) When asked how I built up the Bettmann Archive and achieved a measure of success with this rather offbeat idea, I can think of no element more essential than stick-to-itiveness and relentless application to the task.

Another essential for success in life, I have found, is the meticulous pursuit of order. In this realm we have a mighty preceptor. Did not God himself create order out of chaos? And is not Bach's music the best intimation of the Deity that we have—its logical, orderly development strengthening our resolve to overcome the disorder and confusion we find all around us?

It is my humble philosophy that, in striving for order, we humans try to follow the precepts of the divine. I can't spare my readers another quotation, one that I particularly cherish. The German romantic poet Novalis (Count Friedrich von Hardenberg) once observed, "Chaos always shines through the adornment of order." Life as such is chaotic. It is our task to create order out of it, in whatever tiny niche assigned to us. Order is the quintessential prerequisite for all successful endeavors, whether we write a fugue, bake a pie, build the Parthenon, or found a picture archive.

Thus, my enduring love for the precise, ordered music of the great J. S. is in perfect harmony with my professional predilections. No wonder that I took it as a fine compliment when a perceptive visitor to the Archive—well aware of my musical taste—was moved to comment, "There's a lot of Bach in there."

Walking: the great restorative.

THE READER WILL HAVE deduced by now that I am by nature well suited to be an "inside man"—bending over books or breathing the dust of library stacks. Happily, I have also been endowed (though not athletically constituted) with a great love for the outdoors. Fresh air to me is a form of nourishment as essential as food (or even books). When we had a country home, I spent my weekends outdoors, involving myself strenuously in the shaping of our landscape; weeding, seeding, and crabgrass hunting (the latter a vain pursuit).

I am also a lover and student of trees, which seem to have been produced by nature to provide us with symbols of grace and nobility, patience and endurance. I had grown quite fond of an aged maple tree on our Connecticut property—a maple still proudly upright, though grotesquely gnarled and truncated by the life-preserving work of a tree surgeon. Upon leaving for Florida, I could not help but embrace its scarred trunk, murmuring, "Now you be a good boy and take care of yourself." But if South Florida does not supply such imposing trees as my beloved maple, its subtropical flora has a beauty of its own. Nature always provides.

Resting in Boca Raton's Lyman Lake Park after a stroll. Walking some three miles a day has become for me a health-giving habit.

Communing with nature in various ways is an important component in preserving one's health. As old age has crept up, I have remained an inveterate walker. I consider my perambulating legs to be "assistants to the heart," and the heart—as the very motor of our being—deserves all the assistance we can give it. To preserve one's ambulatory vigor is especially essential as the years pass by. A friend, observing my gait, paid me a compliment the other day: "This Bettmann fellow doesn't walk like an old man." (However flattering that may be, I do not delude myself: the biological clock cannot be defied.)

Whenever possible, I have a brisk walk in one of Boca Raton's lovely parks or tramp along the beach—watching the sea gulls, envious that I cannot write with the ease and grace with which they fly. How to stick to a walker's regimen? One has to establish a routine and make adherence to a schedule automatic, even if one has to resort to threats (such as, "no breakfast today until I finish my three miles"). I assign time every day for my constitutional—a schedule enforced by habit. As a doctor friend of mine warned, "If you do not find time to exercise, then you must find time for a stay in the hospital."

The daily habit of walking is a most pleasurable way of counterbalancing the sedentary pursuits that take up much of my day. Walking is also the ideal way to meditate and to sort out the multitude of tasks ahead (too many, even at my biblical age). I cannot claim this idea is novel or revolutionary. It is only a restatement of a truth the Romans proclaimed long ago: *Mens sana in corpore sano* (A healthy mind can but in a healthy body dwell).

**Life's greatest blessing:
a good wife.**

ENDOWED WITH AN uncommon measure of common sense, my wife, Anne, was always the admired center of our family circle. All critical decisions faced her review as our unquestioned domestic oracle. I remember when I turned 60, I broached to her the idea that I was getting too old and it was about time to sell the business. She replied that I was ready for psychiatric treatment.

Although she did not partake in the Archive's day-to-day doings, no crucial step was ever taken (shall I hire X or retire Y?) without her input. Jokingly, I called her my "Answer Automat." Whenever in a quandary, I grasped a nickel and pointed it toward her temple, as if into a slot in a machine. Her answer was always soundly reasoned, at times prophetic.

On our forty-fourth wedding anniversary, as on all such previous occasions, I sent Anne a "message of the day":

"Forty-four is a pretty good record,
A cloudless time, our lives caringly entwined,
Yours and mine.
Let's not start now to get shifty,
But jointly go for fifty."

Alas, the hopefulness expressed in that makeshift valentine was not to be fulfilled. Shortly thereafter we had to face the fact the Anne had become a victim of macular deterioration, an incurable affliction leading to blindness. She bore this burden heroically, as she did the invasion of the "invisible worm" of cancer, which claimed her life in 1988.

Anne at the wedding of her son
Wendell to Harriet Ruderman.

A glimpse at the picture man's private life.

ALTHOUGH THE CREATION of the Bettmann Archive absorbed much of my time, I was still privileged to enjoy a family life that has added warmth and happiness to my days. When I married Anne in 1938, she brought into our circle her three children: Wendell, Melvin, and Beverly. In the course of years, they have grown as close to me as if they had been my own. I have thoroughly enjoyed the heartwarming affection of the younger set—reflected in this sampling retrieved from the tattered pages of our family album.

Above left: Jonathan Moch, my great-grandson, good-naturedly burlesques my love of books. Even when he was a baby, he showed bibliophilic tendencies—he tried to eat his picture books. Above center: Discussing a paper with one of my granddaughters, Julia Gray, during her medical studies at Brown University in Rhode Island. Above right: An affectionate encounter with Ellen Stolzman, another of my granddaughters. She is now a vice-president at HBO (Time-Warner).

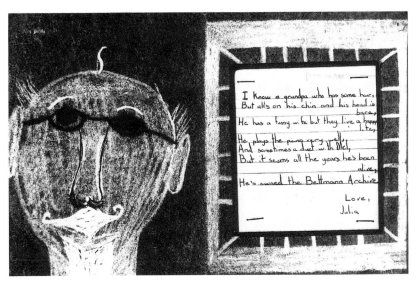

A message from my granddaughter Julia when she was about ten years old. Later a graduate with honors from Brown University Medical School, she now practices obstetrics and gynecology in Stamford, Connecticut. Her juvenile poesy reads:

I know a grandpa who has some hair,
but all's on his chin, and his head is bare.
He has a fussy wife
but they lead a happy life.
He plays the piano very well,
And sometimes a duet with Mel,
But it seems all the years he's been alive,
He's owned the Bettmann Archive.

"Lucky the man who can join the end of his life with its beginning."—J. W. Goethe

THE HAPPY LANDING PLACE I have been granted (in Boca Raton and at FAU) gives a certain symmetry to my long life—a life so crowded with chance happenings and fortuitous turns. I began my professional career among the bibliophilic treasures of the Prussian State Art Library, and I am grateful to live out my final phase among library stacks once again. Thus, my retirement niche lends an elliptical shape to my career—a return to its beginning. I look with satisfaction at this closing of the circle.

Such a pattern is as a rule discernible only after a person's demise. As Hannah Arendt so perceptively put it: "Life becomes a sense-making structure only when it has ended in death. Death not only ends a life, it also bestows on it a silent completeness snatched from the hazardous flux to which all things human are subject."

Having achieved even more than the biblical span of years, I can now see that my life—lived "on the wing" in a succession of apparently chance assignments—has had a logic of its own. This logic has been confirmed by the rich days I spend among the treasures of a university in South Florida—so far in distance and time, so close in purpose and reward, to my beginnings a lifetime ago in Bach's town of Leipzig and the cultural vortex of Berlin.

Though I have had an interesting and productive life, I have not lived with my eyes focused on a *vita eterna*. Rather, I have tried to condition myself to be always aware of the fragility of life and the limits of our tenure on earth. For me, paradise is simply a poetic fancy rather than a reality I can aspire to. However, I do somewhat envy those who have been blessed with the belief that life on earth is but the prologue to an existence of a higher order. Indeed, I admit I find great appeal in the notion that in the longed-for celestial fields nothing but music fills the air. According to orthodox doctrine, the hosts of angels do not speak, but flutter on "wings of song."

Nevertheless, tempting as this prospect is, I rather subscribe to Whitman's idea of death as an end "lovely and soothing" or to Henry James's admission of his "fatigue of life" and his wish for the "sweet peace of nothingness." When Freud meditated about his mother's death, he remarked that her demise was a reward for a life well spent. I hope I will be found worthy of a similar gift.

Hence, the prospect of my departure does not cause me tremors of apprehension. Life is a fugue, and like a Bachian fugue, it is predestined to come to its serene, logical, and liberating end.

"We must so be gone sooner or later all, and as Calliapus in the comedy took his leave of his spectators and auditors (I bid you farewell; clap me when I am gone), must we bid the world farewell . . . having played our part and forever depart."
—Robert Burton, *The Anatomy of Melancholy* (1621).

ACKNOWLEDGMENTS

IN COMPILING THIS BOOK, I had to rely heavily on the resources of the Bettmann Archive, once my daily beat. It was with pleasure that I noticed the agency's continued smooth functioning and astounding growth. Much credit for this accrues to the present director, David Greenstein. His capable lieutenants Peter S. Rohowsky and Katherine G. Bang were unsparing in their solicitude to help. To all of them I express my sincere thanks.

Most fortuitous for me was the "happy landing" I was granted at Florida Atlantic University's Wimberly Library. Its director, Dr. William Miller, assigned to me a fine domain in the Department of Special Collections. This accommodation has worked out well over the years. The library's book and reference collection and complete facilities were accessible to me practically within arm's length. My work on this book was further facilitated by a staff ever ready to help. No bookman could ask for a more inviting ambience.

For guidance and suggestions, I would like to express my thanks to the following individuals: R. Michael Belknap, Maggie Berkvist, Gloria Bock, Zita M. Cael, John Y. Cole, Judith Erickson, Kevin Farmer, David Gottlieb, Margaret Harter, Evelyn Hinrichsen, Alma Kalfus, Ernest Kroll, George Meyerson, Gregory Pluin, John Tebell, Bradbury Thompson, Margaret Vanhove, Mark Van Vliet, Dr. Richard Watt, and Shanon Shuback.

All illustrations in this book are from Bettman (UPI and Reuters Photo Libraries), with the exception of family pictures and photographs from the following agencies, museums, and individuals: cover and frontispiece, Michael O'Connor; pp. 7, 15, Deutsche Fotothek; p. 17, Husserl Archive; pp. 18, 19, C. F. Peters Archive; p. 20 (right), National Gallerie, Berlin; p. 29, Fogg Art Museum, Cambridge, Mass.; p. 45, Skip Sheffield; p. 52 (top), Book-of-the-Month Club; p. 52 (bottom), Robert E. Abrams; p. 61 (left), Eastman House, Rochester, New York; p. 65 (left), *New Yorker*; pp. 148, 152, William Watkins; p. 163 (left), *Boca Raton* magazine; p. 167, Dianne Skafte.

INDEX

Italic page numbers indicate illustrations.